The Kabbalah of
The First Epistle of John
Chapter 5

An Esoteric Exposition
The Alternate Translation Bible (ATB)

For My Parents
Louis and Evelyn Goldstein

Copyright © 2014 by Christ-Centered Kabbalah
All rights reserved under International Copyright Law.
Published @ Long Island, NY November 14, 2014

ISBN: 13: 978-0692333105
ISBN: 10: 069233310X

**The Kabbalah Of The First Epistle Of John
Chapter 5**
Sheila R. Vitale

No part of this book may be reproduced, in any form, without written permission from the publisher

Requests for permission to reproduce selections from this book should be mailed to:

Christ-Centered Kabbalah
Sheila R. Vitale
P O Box 562
Port Jefferson Station, NY 11776-0562 USA
(631) 331-1493

TABLE OF AUTHORITIES

1. **Brown Driver & Briggs' Hebrew Lexicon**, Woodside Bible Fellowship, Ontario, Canada, Licensed From The Institute for Creation Research.

2. **Englishman's Greek-Hebrew Concordance**.

3. **Gesenius' Hebrew and Chaldee Lexicon to the Old Testament** Scriptures, Baker Book House, Grand Rapids, Michigan.

4. **The Interlinear Bible** (Jay P. Green, Sr.), Hendrickson Publisher's, Peabody, Massachusetts 01961-3473.

5. **The Interlinear Bible (transliterated), Biblesoft and International Bible Translators, Inc**.

6. **Nave's Topical Bible**.

7. **Nelson's Bible Dictionary**, Thomas Nelson, Inc., Publishers, Nashville, Tennessee.

8. **Strong's Exhaustive Concordance** (James Strong) Thomas Nelson, Inc., Publishers, Nashville, Tennessee.

9. **Strong's Hebrew And Chaldee Dictionary** (James Strong), Thomas Nelson, Inc., Publishers, Nashville, Tennessee.

10. **Strong's Greek Dictionary** (James Strong), Thomas Nelson, Inc., Publishers, Nashville, Tennessee.

11. **The New Thayer's Greek-English Lexicon Of The New Testament**, Hendrickson Publisher's, Peabody, Massachusetts 01961-3473.

12. **Unger's Bible Dictionary** (Merrill F. Unger), The Moody Bible Institute of Chicago, Chicago, Illinois 60610.

13. **1979 Authorized Version** (AV), The On-Line Bible

14. **Stephanus Greek Text**, The On-Line Bible

15. **Green's Literal Translation**, The On-Line Bible

The Kabbalah of The First Epistle of John Chapter 5

An Esoteric Exposition
The Alternate Translation Bible (ATB)

Translated, Compiled, Edited and Adapted as a Book by Sheila R. Vitale

The Kabbalah of
The First Epistle of John
Chapter 5

Was rendered in Part 4 of **CCK Message #607,** *The Unity of God in Creation (the 13th of the 14 Precepts),* Which Was Transcribed and Edited For Clarity, Continuity of Thought, And Punctuation by
The **CCK** Transcribing and Editing Team

Christ-Centered Kabbalah
~ The Compleat Kabbalah ~
Sheila R. Vitale
Pastor, Teacher & Founder

Ministry Staff
Anthony Milton, Teacher (South Carolina)
Brooke Paige, Teacher (New York)
Sandra Aldrich (MN) (July 7, 1975 – April 28, 2021)

Administrative Staff
Susan Panebianco, Office Manager

Editorial Staff
Rose Herczeg, Editor

Technical Staff
Lape Mobolaji-Lawal, Database Administrator

Ministry Illustrators
Cecilia H. Bryant (Oct. 18, 1921 – Oct. 23, 2013)
Fidelis Onwubueke

Music Staff
June Eble, Singer, Lyricist and Clarinetist
(July 20, 1931 – Jan. 24, 2024)
Don Gervais, Singer, Lyricist and Guitarist
Rita L. Rora, Singer, Lyricist and Guitarist

Table of Contents

THE KABBALAH OF 1ST JOHN CHAPTER 5

PREFACE I

    WHY ANOTHER TRANSLATION? I
    PREPARING TO TRANSLATE III
    ALTERNATE TRANSLATIONS ARE PROGRESSIVE IV
    THE TORAH (THE WORD OF GOD) IS ALIVE IV

KING JAMES TRANSLATION 1

ALTERNATE TRANSLATION 5

    SPIRITUAL COMPLETION 5
    ATTACHED TO GOD 5
    THE LOVE OF GOD 6
    OUR FAITH 6
    OVERCOMING THE FALLEN NATURE 6
    JOSEPH & ABRAHAM 6
    THREE WITNESSES IN HEAVEN 6
    THREE WITNESSES IN THE EARTH 7
    JESUS GREATER THAN MOSES 7
    ETERNAL LIFE IS IN JESUS CHRIST 7
    CHRIST IN YOU 7
    TRUE WITNESS, FALSE WITNESS 7
    THE NATURE OF GOD 8
    GOD HEARS OUR PRAYERS 8
    ACCORDING TO HIS WILL 8
    REMISSION OF SIN 8
    REPENTANCE 8
    CHRIST CANNOT SIN 9
    THE POWER TO FORGIVE SINS 9
    JESUS, THE ONLY REALITY 9
    GOD IS INSIDE OF US 9
    IDOLS IN THE HEART 10

ANNOTATED ALTERNATE TRANSLATION (ATB) 13

SPIRITUAL COMPLETION	13
ATTACHED TO GOD	14
THE LOVE OF GOD	14
OUR FAITH	14
OVERCOMING THE FALLEN NATURE	14
JOSEPH & ABRAHAM	15
THREE WITNESSES IN HEAVEN	15
THREE WITNESSES IN THE EARTH	16
JESUS GREATER THAN MOSES	16
ETERNAL LIFE IS IN JESUS CHRIST	17
CHRIST IN YOU	17
TRUE WITNESS, FALSE WITNESS	17
THE NATURE OF GOD	17
GOD HEARS OUR PRAYERS	18
ACCORDING TO HIS WILL	18
REMISSION OF SIN FOR THE IGNORANT	18
REPENTANCE FOR THE SONS	18
CHRIST DOES NOT SIN	19
THE POWER TO FORGIVE SINS	19
JESUS, THE ONLY REALITY	19
GOD IS INSIDE OF US	20
IDOLS IN THE HEART	20

APPENDIX – VERSE 1 .... **23**

   REFERENCE SCRIPTURES FOR VERSE 1 23
   FOOTNOTES FOR VERSE 1 25

APPENDIX - VERSE 2 .... **42**

   REFERENCE SCRIPTURES FOR VERSE 2 42

APPENDIX – VERSE 3 .... **45**

   REFERENCE SCRIPTURES FOR VERSE 3 45

APPENDIX – VERSE 4 .... **46**

   REFERENCE SCRIPTURES FOR VERSE 4 46

APPENDIX – VERSE 5 .... **47**

   REFERENCE SCRIPTURES FOR VERSE 5 47

APPENDIX – VERSE 6 .... **48**

   REFERENCE SCRIPTURES FOR VERSE 6 48
   FOOTNOTES FOR VERSE 6 49

APPENDIX – VERSE 7 .... **62**

REFERENCE SCRIPTURES FOR VERSE 7	62
FOOTNOTES FOR VERSE 7	64
APPENDIX – VERSE 8	**70**
REFERENCE SCRIPTURES FOR VERSE 8	70
FOOTNOTES FOR VERSE 8	71
APPENDIX – VERSE 9	**74**
REFERENCE SCRIPTURES FOR VERSE 9	74
APPENDIX – VERSE 10	**76**
REFERENCE SCRIPTURES FOR VERSE 10	76
APPENDIX – VERSE 11	**77**
REFERENCE SCRIPTURES FOR VERSE 11	77
APPENDIX – VERSE 12	**78**
REFERENCE SCRIPTURES FOR VERSE 12	78
APPENDIX – VERSE 13	**79**
REFERENCE SCRIPTURES FOR VERSE 13	79
APPENDIX – VERSE 14	**81**
REFERENCE SCRIPTURES FOR VERSE 14	81
APPENDIX – VERSE 15	**82**
APPENDIX – VERSE 16A	**83**
REFERENCE SCRIPTURES FOR VERSE 16A	83
APPENDIX – VERSE 16B	**84**
REFERENCE SCRIPTURES FOR VERSE 16B	84
APPENDIX – VERSE 17	**86**
REFERENCE SCRIPTURES FOR VERSE 17	86
APPENDIX - VERSE 18	**87**
REFERENCE SCRIPTURES FOR VERSE 18	87
APPENDIX – VERSE 19	**88**
REFERENCE SCRIPTURES FOR VERSE 19	88
APPENDIX - VERSE 20	**90**
REFERENCE SCRIPTURES FOR VERSE 20	90

APPENDIX - VERSE 21 91
    REFERENCE SCRIPTURES FOR VERSE 21 91
TABLE OF REFERENCES 95
ABOUT THE AUTHOR 97

The Alternate Translation Bible©

The Alternate Translation Bible (ATB) is an original translation of the Scripture.

Alternate Translation of the Old Testament©
Alternate Translation, Exodus, Chapter 32
    (Crime of the Calf)©
Alternate Translation, Daniel, Chapter 8©
Alternate Translation, Daniel, Chapter 11©

Alternate Translation of the New Testament©
Alternate Translation, 2 Thessalonians, Chapter 2
    (Sophia)©
Alternate Translation, 1st John, Chapter 5©
Alternate Translation, the Book of Colossians
    (To The Church At Colosse)
Alternate Translation, the Book of Corinthians, Chapter 11
    (Corinthian Confusion)
Alternate Translation, the Book of Jude
    (The Common Salvation)©

Alternate Translation of the Book of the Revelation of Jesus
    Christ to St. John©
Traducción Alternada del Libro de Revelación de Jesucristo©

Alternate Translations in This Book

GEN 2:23-25	30
MK 5:32-34	34
HEB 2:16	52
JER 22:29-30	55
MATT 13:8 AND 23	56
GEN 49:10	58
1 KINGS 8:25	60

The Kabbalah of
The First Epistle of John
Chapter 5

An Esoteric Exposition
The Alternate Translation Bible (ATB)

Preface

Why Another Translation?

The King James Translators were not spiritual men. They were scholars who, themselves, perceived the Deity of the Scripture as an unforgiving, punishing God. But there is another Message, a spiritual understanding of the Scripture called *the Doctrine of Christ*, which reveals a loving God, whose sole intention towards mankind is to deliver us from destruction and death.

There are many definitions for each word in the English dictionary, and many translations for each Hebrew and Greek word in the original text of the Scripture.

The King James Translators dealt with the problem of one Hebrew source word appearing several times in a single Chapter, by using a different English word each time that the Hebrew word appears. The English word choices of the translator, then, are directly related to 1) his knowledge of the Word of God, 2) the degree to which he is influenced by the Spirit of Revelation and 3) the accepted understanding of the Word of God at the time.

The Spirit of Revelation influences the translator to choose legitimate *Alternate Translations* from the Hebrew and Greek lexicons listed in the front of *The Prophecies of Daniel According to Kabbalah, Chapter 8, Alternate Translation*, to express the spiritual intent of the Scripture. The Alternate English Translations for some of the Hebrew words in the Scripture are just as legitimate as the choices made by the King James Translators, but they render a radically different, and much more positive Translation than the Authorized Version.

Multiple English translations for the same Hebrew word in the King James text are perfectly legitimate examples of

Translator's License, and simply prove our point: *The King James Translators, themselves, used multiple definitions of the same Hebrew Word.*

The Prophecies of Daniel According to Kabbalah, Chapter 8, is a Spiritual Translation of the Scripture, which is as legitimate to the Spiritual Mind, as the King James translation is to the Carnal Mind. The *Alternate Translation Bi*ble sounds radically different than the King James and other translations, because it must be Spiritually Discerned (1 Cor. 2:14).

A knowledge of the True Intent of the author of the Scripture, and a desire to understand the message that he intended to convey, should be the top priority for all genuine seekers of *Truth*.

God is the Living Word that feeds Mankind through imperfect vessels. Beware of idolatry for the King James, or any other Translation, because *all translations* are the work of imperfect, mortal men. Seek God and He will direct your paths (Pro. 3:6).

May the Spirit of Truth expose all of our wrong thinking, and may the Truth intended by the author of the Word cleave to our heart and mind, because the Spirit of Truth awakens our potential for Eternal Life (1 Cor 15:4).

Romans 8:1-14

1. THERE IS THEREFORE NOW NO CONDEMNATION TO THEM WHICH ARE IN CHRIST JESUS, WHO WALK NOT AFTER THE FLESH, BUT AFTER THE SPIRIT.

2. FOR THE LAW OF THE SPIRIT OF LIFE IN CHRIST JESUS HATH MADE ME FREE FROM THE LAW OF SIN AND DEATH.

3. FOR WHAT THE LAW COULD NOT DO, IN THAT IT WAS WEAK THROUGH THE FLESH, GOD SENDING HIS OWN SON IN THE LIKENESS OF SINFUL FLESH, AND FOR SIN, CONDEMNED SIN IN THE FLESH:

4. THAT THE RIGHTEOUSNESS OF THE LAW MIGHT BE FULFILLED IN US, WHO WALK NOT AFTER THE FLESH, BUT AFTER THE SPIRIT.

5.   FOR THEY THAT ARE AFTER THE FLESH DO MIND THE THINGS OF THE FLESH; BUT THEY THAT ARE AFTER THE SPIRIT THE THINGS OF THE SPIRIT.

6.   FOR TO BE CARNALLY MINDED IS DEATH; BUT TO BE SPIRITUALLY MINDED IS LIFE AND PEACE.

7.   BECAUSE THE CARNAL MIND IS ENMITY AGAINST GOD: FOR IT IS NOT SUBJECT TO THE LAW OF GOD, NEITHER INDEED CAN BE.

8.   SO THEN THEY THAT ARE IN THE FLESH CANNOT PLEASE GOD.

9.   BUT YE ARE NOT IN THE FLESH, BUT IN THE SPIRIT, IF SO BE THAT THE SPIRIT OF GOD DWELL IN YOU. NOW IF ANY MAN HAVE NOT THE SPIRIT OF CHRIST, HE IS NONE OF HIS.

10. AND IF CHRIST BE IN YOU, THE BODY IS DEAD BECAUSE OF SIN; BUT THE SPIRIT IS LIFE BECAUSE OF RIGHTEOUSNESS.

11. BUT IF THE SPIRIT OF HIM THAT RAISED UP JESUS FROM THE DEAD DWELL IN YOU, HE THAT RAISED UP CHRIST FROM THE DEAD SHALL ALSO QUICKEN YOUR MORTAL BODIES BY HIS SPIRIT THAT DWELLETH IN YOU.

12. THEREFORE, BRETHREN, WE ARE DEBTORS, NOT TO THE FLESH, TO LIVE AFTER THE FLESH.

FOR IF YE LIVE AFTER THE FLESH, YE SHALL DIE: BUT IF YE THROUGH THE SPIRIT DO MORTIFY THE DEEDS OF THE BODY, YE SHALL LIVE.

Preparing To Translate

The Prophesies of Daniel According to Kabbalah, Chapter 8, Alternate Translation, was researched in March of 2015, and preached in two separate meetings as *Christ-Centered Kabbalah* Message #831, *A History of Adam.*

Three Hebrew-English dictionaries, three Interlinear Texts, and multiple Bible Dictionaries (see, Table of Authorities at the beginning of *this Book*) were used to search out the meaning of each Hebrew word of Daniel, Chapter 8. English dictionaries, encyclopedias and search engines, were also employed to acquire as much information as possible about obviously, and not so obviously related topics, which were revealed through the *Alternate Translations.*

Each word and verse was seriously prayed over to discover God's spiritual message behind the written words.

The Prophecies of Daniel, Chapter 8, Accorcing to Kabbalah, Alternate Translation, contains a Table of References, as well as an Appendix for each verse, which includes the Notes created for that verse as CCK Message #831, *A History of Adam*, was preached.

It is not unusual for the verse structure of the *Alternate Translations* to be rearranged so that they can be read as one continuous message. Accordingly, some paragraph numbers are out of order (*3* before *2*, for example) and some paragraphs are divided into *a* and *b* and interspersed (*2a, 3a, 2b, 3b,* for example).

Alternate Translations Are Progressive

Alternate Translations were rendered for each verse in its entirety. After that, all of the translated verses are read together as one whole revelation, to confirm their synchronicity, reveal additional, deep nuances of the whole revelation, and to expose any inconsistencies or errors.

Alternate Translations are progressive in that the *Alternate Translation* for each verse is affected by the *Alternate Translations* for previous and subsequent verses. A newly translated verse, for example, will be influenced by previous Alternate Translations, and sometimes the Alternate Translation for the new verse causes changes in previously translated verses.

The Torah (The Word of God) Is Alive

The *Alternate Translation* of one whole chapter of Scripture is a living organism that evolves and grows in scope. The Spirit of Revelation refines the *Alternate Translations* as the translator reads and re-reads them. Eventually, all of the thoughts, understanding and influences of the Carnal Mind are removed, and the optimal understanding for that particular time, is reached.

Accordingly, you will find several versions of *Daniel, Chapter 8*, in this Book, which represent the progression of the *Alternate Translation* from its beginning to its final stage:

1. The King James Version [KJV]
2. The Alternate, Amplified Translation [ATB]
3. The Alternate Amplified Translation – Annotated [ATB]

Written words are vessels that clothe the spiritual word, just like the body is a vessel that carries the soul in this world. It might even be said that the spiritual understanding of a written word is the soul of that written word.

Unveiling the spiritual meaning of a word shatters its hard exterior, so that the spiritual contents flow out and blend with the spiritual contents of the other vessels. *The Spirit of Revelation* takes hold of the Torah (Word of God) in this *liquid form*, goes beyond the letter of the Word, and reveals the esoteric message of the Torah (Word of God) for a particular people, at an appointed time.

Sheila R. Vitale

1st John, Chapter 5
King James Translation

The Kabbalah of The First Epistle of John Chapter 5
An Esoteric Exposition

King James Translation

¹ Whosoever believeth that Jesus is the Christ is born of God: and every one that loveth him that begat loveth him also that is begotten of him.

² By this we know that we love the children of God, when we love God, and keep his commandments.

³ For this is the love of God, that we keep his commandments: and his commandments are not grievous.

⁴ For whatsoever is born of God overcometh the world: and this is the victory that overcometh the world, even our faith.

⁵ Who is he that overcometh the world, but he that believeth that Jesus is the Son of God?

⁶ This is he that came by water and blood, even Jesus Christ; not by water only, but by water and blood. And it is the Spirit that beareth witness, because the Spirit is truth.

⁷ For there are three that bear record in heaven, the Father, the Word, and the Holy Ghost: and these three are one.

⁸ And there are three that bear witness in earth, the spirit, and the water, and the blood: and these three agree in one.

⁹ If we receive the witness of men, the witness of God is greater: for this is the witness of God which he hath testified of his Son.

¹⁰ He that believeth on the Son of God hath the witness in himself: he that believeth not God hath made him a liar; because he believeth not the record that God gave of his Son.

¹¹ And this is the record, that God hath given to us eternal life, and this life is in his Son.

¹² He that hath the Son hath life; and he that hath not the Son of God hath not life.

¹³ These things have I written unto you that believe on the name of the Son of God; that ye may know that ye have eternal life, and that ye may believe on the name of the Son of God.

¹⁴ And this is the confidence that we have in him, that, if we ask any thing according to his will, he heareth us:

¹⁵ And if we know that he hear us, whatsoever we ask, we know that we have the petitions that we desired of him.

¹⁶ If any man see his brother sin a sin which is not unto death, he shall ask, and he shall give him life for them that sin not unto death. There is a sin unto death: I do not say that he shall pray for it.

¹⁷ All unrighteousness is sin: and there is a sin not unto death.

¹⁸ We know that whosoever is born of God sinneth not; but he that is begotten of God keepeth himself, and that wicked one toucheth him not.

¹⁹ And we know that we are of God, and the whole world lieth in wickedness.

²⁰ And we know that the Son of God is come, and hath given us an understanding, that we may know him that is true, and we are in him that is true, even in his Son Jesus Christ. This is the true God, and eternal life.

²¹ Little children, keep yourselves from idols. Amen.

Alternate Translation
1ˢᵗ John, Chapter 5

ALTERNATE TRANSLATION

The Kabbalah of The First Epistle of John
Chapter 5
An Esoteric Exposition

Alternate Translation (ATB)

Rendered in Part 4 of CCK Message # 607,
The Unity of God in Creation
(The 13th of 14 Precepts)

Spiritual Completion

5.01 [Whoever is] complete believes that Jesus is the regenerated Christ of God, and is attached to the regenerated [first Adam, and is] also attached [to Christ in] whoever [Jesus has] regenerated him,

Attached To God

5.02 And this is how we disciples know that we are attached to God: When we are attached to God, we keep his commandments,

ALTERNATE TRANSLATION

The Love Of God

5.03   Because God [demonstrated his] love for us [when he gave us his] commandments, and keeping his commandments is not a hardship [when his son is born in us],

Our Faith

5.04   Because, when God regenerates the whole [Adam], he subdues the [spiritual] world [within himself], and he succeeds [in subduing] this [spiritual world] through [the Lord Jesus Christ, the beginning and end of] our faith.

Overcoming The Fallen Nature

5.05   Whose [spiritual seminal fluid provides the seed that] subdues the world [of our fallen nature], unless we do not believe that Jesus is the Son of God,

Joseph & Abraham

5.06   [Because] Jesus Christ is the one who came into existence by the spirit[ually female seed of] the seminal fluid [of Joseph, the son of David], and by [the male] spirit[ual] blood [seed of Abraham]; not only by [the spiritually female seed of] the seminal fluid of [Joseph, the son of David], but by [the spiritually female seed of] the seminal fluid [of Joseph, the son of David] *AND* [the male spiritual] blood [seed of Abraham]; and the Spirit of Truth is [one of]

Three Witnesses In Heaven

5.07   The three witnesses in heaven that [Jesus is the Son of God]: The **Father, the Word *[of God]*, and the Holy Spirit**, and these three [comprise ***Ancient Adam***, who is] one, whole [spiritual man, and]

ALTERNATE TRANSLATION

Three Witnesses In The Earth

5.08   There are three that bear witness in the earth [that Jesus is the Son of God, the human] spirit, [the spiritually female seed of] the seminal fluid [of Joseph, the son of David], and the [spiritual] blood [seed of Abraham], and these three [comprise Christ Jesus, who is] one [whole spiritual man].

Jesus Greater Than Moses

5.09   [Now, if] we believe the evidence [that God gave to prove that Moses was] a completed man, [we should also believe] the evidence [that] God [gave to prove that Jesus is greater than Moses], and this is the evidence that God has presented with respect to his Son:

Eternal Life Is In Jesus Christ

5.11   God has given us eternal life and that life is in [Jesus Christ], his Son, and this is the evidence: [that God has given us eternal life through Jesus Christ]:

Christ In You

5.12   Whoever is possessed by [Christ Jesus], the Son [of Jesus Christ], has [eternal] life, and whoever is not possessed by [Christ Jesus, the Son of Jesus Christ], the Son of God, does not have eternal life; [and],

True Witness, False Witness

5.10   Whoever believes [that Jesus Christ is] the Son of God, is possessed by [Christ Jesus], *the witness of God within himself*; but [the personality] that does not believe [that Jesus Christ is the Son of] God, is possessed by [Satan and Leviathan, their carnal mind], *the false witness* [that God is] within himself,

ALTERNATE TRANSLATION

[because the carnal mind of fallen Adam] does not believe the evidence that God testified to [concerning] his Son,

The Nature Of God

5.13   I have written these things to you [who] believe [that it is possible to acquire Christ], the nature, of the Son of God, to help you to become intimate [with the Lord Jesus Christ], the Son of God, [who is the way we begin to attain] eternal life through [Christ], the nature of [God, and

God Hears Our Prayers

5.14   When we have the nature of God within us], we are bold enough [to believe] that [the Father] hears us when we ask for anything that is according to his Will, and

According To His Will

5.15   We know that if [the Father] hears everything that we ask for, we [also] know that we will receive everything that we desire [that is according to his Will for us];

Remission Of Sin

5.16a   [So], if anyone sees his brother sin a sin that does not call for capital punishment, and he asks [the Father to pardon that man, the Father] will give life to [that man whose] sin does not call for capital punishment. [However], there is a sin that calls for capital punishment, and I am clearly telling you not to pray for [the man who is guilty] of it.

Repentance

5.16b   [Also], if any one perceives that his brother [who] has been granted [eternal] life, [might be] sinning a sin that could result in the death [of the resurrected Christ within himself, and reveals it to him], and [the son of God] asks [to be forgiven] he will not die, [but you should know that] instructing [the sinner who will not repent, and] praying for him, will not [stop Satan], his sin nature [who is the enforcer of Jehovah's righteous Sowing & Reaping Judgment, from bestowing] death upon him.

Christ Cannot Sin

5.18   We know that [Christ, the one who] is born of God, does not sin, but, on the contrary, [Christ, the one who] God has begotten, guards [Abel, his other self, against Cain, the daughter of Satan], the evil one, [who desires] to engage in spiritual sexual intercourse of the mind with [him];

The Power To Forgive Sins

5.17   [Nevertheless], everything that is unjust and unfair is sin, [and all sin is punishable by death], but sometimes sin does not result in death [when you repent and Christ Jesus forgives your sin].

Jesus, The Only Reality

15.19   [Now], we know that all [the denizens of] the world [of Yetzirah,, the Astral Plane], where the unclean spirits and demons] are lying [in bed with Satan], the evil one, but we [also] know that the Son of God is come, and [that] he has given us the understanding that Jesus Christ, the Son of God, is the only one who is true, and that we are a part of his reality, which is the eternal life of God, [and]

God Is Inside Of Us

5.20   We [also] know that [the reason that] the Son of God has come, and has given us understanding, [is] that we may know the Truth, and the Truth is that [Christ Jesus], the Son of

Jesus Christ, is in[side of] us, and that this [Christ Jesus] is the [only] genuine [source of] the eternal life of God.

Idols In The Heart

5.21 [Wherefore, brethren], may [Christ Jesus] guard all of you [spiritual] children from [Satan and Leviathan, your carnal mind, which are] the idols [in your heart].

ANNOTATED
ALTERNATE TRANSLATION
1ST JOHN, CHAPTER 5

The Kabbalah of The First Epistle of John
Chapter 5
An Esoteric Exposition

Annotated Alternate Translation (ATB)

Spiritual Completion

5.01 [Whoever is] complete [1] [R-1] believes that Jesus is the regenerated Christ[R-2] of God, [2] and is attached to the regenerated [first Adam, [R-3] and is] also attached [to Christ in] whoever [Jesus has] regenerated [R-4] him,

[R-1] Col 2:10
[R-2] 1 Cor 15:4
[R-3] 1 Cor 15:45
[R-4] Matt 19:28

---

[1] **To be complete** is a translation of a Greek word that means **all**, or **whole**. **Completion** signifies a male and a female part. (See complete footnote in Appendix #1, p. 20.)

[2] The Greek word translated **Christ**, is a general, impersonal word that means **anointed**. (See complete footnote in Appendix #2, p. 21.)

Attached To God

5.02   And this is how we disciples know that we are attached [R-1] to God: When we are attached to God, we keep his commandments,[R-2]

[R-1] Mal 1:2-3
[R-2] Ex 20:1-17

The Love Of God

5.03   Because God [demonstrated his] love for us [when he gave us his] commandments, and keeping his commandments is not a hardship [when his son is born [R] in us],

[R] Rev 12:5

Our Faith

5.04   Because, when God regenerates the whole [Adam], he subdues the [spiritual] world [within himself], and he succeeds [in subduing] this [spiritual world] through [the Lord Jesus Christ, the beginning and end of] our faith;[R]

[R] Heb 12:2

Overcoming The Fallen Nature

5.05   Whose [spiritual seminal fluid provides the seed that] subdues the world [of our fallen nature], unless we do not believe that Jesus is the Son of God,[R]

[R] Rom 11:20

ANNOTATED ALTERNATE TRANSLATION

Joseph & Abraham

5.06   [Because] Jesus Christ is the one who came into existence by the spirit[ually female seed [3] of] the seminal fluid [of Joseph, the son of David],[4] [R-1] and by [the male] spirit[ual] blood [seed of Abraham];[R-2] not only by [the spiritually female seed of] the seminal fluid of [Joseph, the son of David],[R-1] but by [the spiritually female seed of] the seminal fluid [of Joseph, the son of David][R-1] *AND* [the male spiritual] blood [seed of Abraham]; [R-2] and the Spirit of Truth[R-3] is [one of]

[R-1] Lk 3:23
[R-2] Gal 3:16
[R-3] Jn 1:17

Three Witnesses In Heaven

5.07   The three witnesses in heaven that [Jesus is the Son of God]:[R-1] *the Father*,[5] [R-2] *the Word [of God]*, [6] [R-3] and *the Holy*

---

[3]   How can the female seed of a human male produce a male, physical child? The answer is that all of humanity is spiritually female in relation to God,... (See complete footnote in Appendix #3, p. 44.)

[4]   The English words, *as supposed*, in the King James Translation of Lk 3:23, are a translation of two Greek words which mean, *according to the commonly accepted custom*. (See complete footnote in Appendix #4, p. 44.)

[5]   *The Father* is the personality associated with the Sefirah, *Chochmah*, and his attribute is *Wisdom*:... (See complete footnote in Appendix #5, p. 58.)

[6]   *The Word of God* is *Ancient Adam*. The Kabbalists call him *Adam Kadmon, Primordial human*. (See complete footnote in Appendix #6, p. 60.)

***Spirit*,** [7] [R-4] and these three [comprise ***Ancient Adam*,**[R-4] who is] one, whole [spiritual man,[R-5] and]

[R-1] Heb 4:14
[R-2] Pro 9:1
[R-3] Rev 19:13
[R-4] Pro 24:3
[R-5] Dan 7:9
[R-6] Acts 17:28

Three Witnesses In The Earth

5.08 There are three that bear witness in the earth [that Jesus is the Son of God, the human] spirit, [8] [R-1] [the spiritually female seed of] the seminal fluid [of Joseph, the son of David],[9] [R-2] and the [spiritual] blood [seed of Abraham],[10] [R-3] and these three [comprise Christ Jesus,[R-4] who is] one [whole spiritual man].

[R-1] Rom 8:15
Gal 4:6
[R-2] Lk 3:23
[R-3] Gal 3:16
[R-4] 1 Tim 2:5

Jesus Greater Than Moses

5.09 [Now, if] we believe the evidence [that God gave to prove that Moses [R-1] was] a completed man,[R-2] [we should also

---

[7] **The Holy Spirit** that John references here comes from the third Sefirah called Binah. Her attribute is **Understanding** and her personality is **Mother**. (See complete footnote in Appendix #7, p. 61.)

[8] **The human spirit** in a man is the Shekinah in captivity. (See complete footnote in Appendix #8, p. 65.)

[9] **The human spirit** and the female side of the spiritual seed of the Father are the Shekinah. (See complete footnote in Appendix #9, p. 66.)

[10] **Christ in Jesus is a witness that Jesus is the Son of God**, because Christ rose from the dead in the man, Jesus:... (See complete footnote in Appendix #10, p. 67.)

ANNOTATED ALTERNATE TRANSLATION

believe] the evidence [that] God [gave to prove that Jesus is greater than Moses], and this is the evidence that God has presented with respect to his Son:

R-1 Ex 7:14-18
R-2 Col 2:10

Eternal Life Is In Jesus Christ

5.11   God has given us eternal life ^{R-1} and that life is in [Jesus Christ], his Son, ^{R-2} and this is the evidence: [that God has given us eternal life through Jesus Christ]:

R-1 Jn 17:3
R-2 Jn 6:54

Christ In You ^{R-1}

5.12   Whoever is possessed by [Christ Jesus], the Son [of Jesus Christ], has [eternal] life,^{R-2} and whoever is not possessed by [Christ Jesus, the Son of Jesus Christ], the Son of God, does not have eternal life; [and],

R-1 Col 1:27
R-2 Jn 10:28
Rom 6:23

True Witness, False Witness

5.10   Whoever believes [that Jesus Christ is] the Son of God, is possessed by [Christ Jesus], *the witness of God within himself*; but [the personality] that does not believe [that Jesus Christ is the Son of] God, is possessed by [Satan and Leviathan, their carnal mind], *the false witness* ^R [that God is] within himself, [because the carnal mind of fallen Adam] does not believe the evidence that God testified to [concerning] his Son,

R 1 Thess 2:11

The Nature Of God

5.13   I have written these things to you [who] believe [that it is possible to acquire Christ ^{R-1}], the nature,^{R-2} of the Son of God, to help you to become intimate [with the Lord Jesus Christ],

ANNOTATED ALTERNATE TRANSLATION

the Son of God, [who is the way ^{R-3} we begin to attain] eternal life through [Christ ^{R-1}], the nature of [God, ^{R-2} and

^{R-1} Gal 3:16
Col 1:27
^{R-2} 2 Pet 1:4
^{R-3} Jn 14:6

God Hears Our Prayers

5.14   When we have the nature ^{R-1} of God within us], we are bold enough [to believe] that [the Father] hears ^{R-2} us when we ask for anything that is according to his Will,^{R-3} and

^{R-1} 2 Pet 1:4
^{R-2} Jn 9:31
^{R-3} Lk 22:42

According To His Will

5.15   We know that if [the Father] hears everything that we ask for, we [also] know that we will receive everything that we desire [that is according to his Will for us];

Remission of Sin For The Ignorant ^{R-1}

5.16a   [So], if anyone sees his brother sin a sin that does not call for capital punishment, and he asks [the Father to pardon that man,^{R-2} the Father] will give life ^{R-3} to [that man whose] sin does not call for capital punishment. [However], there is a sin that calls for capital punishment, and I am clearly telling you not to pray for [the man who is guilty] of it.

^{R-1} Lk 12:48
^{R-2} Jn 20:23
^{R-3} Jn 10:10

Repentance For The Sons

5.16b   [Also], if any one perceives that his brother ^{R-1} [who] has been granted [eternal] life, [might be] sinning a sin that could result in the death [of the resurrected Christ within himself, and reveals it to him], and [the son of God] asks [to be forgiven] he will not die, ^{R-2} [but you should know that] instructing [the sinner who will not repent, and] praying for him, will not [stop Satan], his sin nature [who is the enforcer of Jehovah's righteous Sowing & Reaping Judgment, from bestowing] death upon him.[R-3]

[R-1] Matt 12:50
[R-2] Jn 20:23
[R-3] Heb 6:4-6

Christ Does Not Sin

5.18   We know that [Christ, the one who] is born of God, [R-1] does not sin, but, on the contrary, [Christ, the one who] God has begotten, [R-2] guards [Abel, his other self, against Cain, the daughter of Satan], the evil one,[R-3] [who desires] to engage in spiritual sexual intercourse of the mind with [him];

[R-1] Heb 5:5
[R-2] Heb 11:7
[R-3] Rev 18:9

The Power to Forgive Sins [R-1]

5.17   [Nevertheless], everything that is unjust and unfair is sin, [and all sin is punishable by death],[R-2] but sometimes sin does not result in death [when you repent and Christ Jesus forgives your sin].[R-2]

[R-1] Lk 5:24
[R-2] Rom 6:23
[R-1] Jn 20:23

Jesus, The Only Reality

15.19   [Now], we know that all [the denizens of] the world [of Yetzirah, the Astral Plane], where the unclean spirits and demons] [R-1] are lying [in bed with Satan], the evil one,[R-2] but we [also] know that the Son of God is come, and [that] he has given us the understanding that Jesus Christ, the Son of God, is the only one who is true,^{R-3} and that we are a part of his reality, ^{R4} which is the eternal life of God, ^{R-5} [and]

^{R-1} Matt 12:43
^{R-2} Rev 18:9
^{R-3} Jn 14:6
Rev 3:14
^{R-4} Col 1:8
^{R-5} 1 Tim 6:15

God Is Inside Of Us

5.20   We [also] know that [the reason that] the Son of God has come, and has given us understanding, [is] that we may know the Truth, ^{R-1} and the Truth is that [Christ Jesus], the Son of Jesus Christ, is in[side^{R-2} of] us, and that this [Christ Jesus] is the [only] genuine [source of] the eternal life of God. ^{R-3}

^{R-1} Jn 8:32
^{R-2} Lk 17:21
^{R-3} 1 Tim 6:15

Idols In The Heart

5.21   [Wherefore, brethren], may [Christ Jesus] guard all of you [spiritual] children from [Satan and Leviathan, your carnal mind, which are] the idols [in your heart].^R

^R Ex 14:7

APPENDICES

APPENDIX – Verse 1

Reference Scriptures for Verse 1

R-1 Col 2:10
* R-2 1 Cor 15:4
* R-3 1 Cor 15:45
R-4 Matt 19:28

Col 2:10

^{10}AND YE ARE COMPLETE IN HIM, WHICH IS THE HEAD OF ALL PRINCIPALITY AND POWER:

KJV

1 Cor 15:4

^{4}AND THAT HE WAS BURIED, AND THAT HE ROSE AGAIN THE THIRD DAY ACCORDING TO THE SCRIPTURES:

KJV

1 Cor 15:45

^{45}AND SO IT IS WRITTEN, THE FIRST MAN ADAM WAS MADE A LIVING SOUL; THE LAST ADAM WAS MADE A QUICKENING SPIRIT.

KJV

Matt 19:28

²⁸AND JESUS SAID UNTO THEM, VERILY I SAY UNTO YOU, THAT YE WHICH HAVE FOLLOWED ME, IN THE REGENERATION WHEN THE SON OF MAN SHALL SIT IN THE THRONE OF HIS GLORY, YE ALSO SHALL SIT UPON TWELVE THRONES, JUDGING THE TWELVE TRIBES OF ISRAEL.

KJV

Footnotes for Verse 1

Footnote #1

Spiritual Completion

To be complete is a translation of a Greek word that means ***all***, or ***whole***. ***Completion*** signifies a male and a female part. Adam of creation ceased to be complete, or whole, after Jehovah divided him from his adulterous wife . . .

Gen 2:22

²²AND THE RIB, WHICH THE LORD GOD HAD TAKEN FROM MAN, MADE HE A WOMAN, AND BROUGHT HER UNTO THE MAN.

KJV

. . . who had joined herself to the Snake:

Gen 3:2-6

²AND THE WOMAN SAID UNTO THE SERPENT, WE MAY EAT OF THE FRUIT OF THE TREES OF THE GARDEN:

³BUT OF THE FRUIT OF THE TREE WHICH IS IN THE MIDST OF THE GARDEN, GOD HATH SAID, YE SHALL NOT EAT OF IT, NEITHER SHALL YE TOUCH IT, LEST YE DIE.

⁴AND THE SERPENT SAID UNTO THE WOMAN, YE SHALL NOT SURELY DIE:

Appendix – Verse 1

⁵FOR GOD DOTH KNOW THAT IN THE DAY YE EAT THEREOF, THEN YOUR EYES SHALL BE OPENED, AND YE SHALL BE AS GODS, KNOWING GOOD AND EVIL.

⁶*AND WHEN THE WOMAN* SAW THAT THE TREE WAS GOOD FOR FOOD, AND THAT IT WAS PLEASANT TO THE EYES, AND A TREE TO BE DESIRED TO MAKE ONE WISE, SHE *TOOK OF THE FRUIT THEREOF, AND DID EAT, AND GAVE ALSO UNTO HER HUSBAND WITH HER; AND HE DID EAT.*

KJV

Footnote #2

The Christ of God

The Greek word translated **Christ**, is a general, impersonal word that means ***anointed***.

Adam of creation was the ***anointed***, or ***the Christ of* THE AGE OF INNOCENCE.**

Jesus is the ***anointed*, THE CHRIST OF THIS PRESENT AGE.**

The 1st Adam

The Christ of God in the context of Verse 1, alludes to ***the 1st Adam, the Adam of Creation***.

Adam is a two-sided man, male and female . . .

Gen 1:27

²⁷ SO GOD CREATED MAN IN HIS OWN IMAGE, IN THE IMAGE OF GOD CREATED HE HIM; *MALE AND FEMALE CREATED HE THEM.*

KJV

. . . and Adam's female side was adulterous. She was attracted to the Snake, the personality of the emotional waters of the abyss . . .

Gen 3:4-5

⁴ AND THE SERPENT SAID UNTO THE WOMAN, YE SHALL NOT SURELY DIE:

⁵ FOR GOD DOTH KNOW THAT *IN THE DAY YE EAT THEREOF, THEN YOUR EYES SHALL BE OPENED, AND YE SHALL BE AS GODS,* KNOWING GOOD AND EVIL.

KJV

. . . and joined herself to them while she was still married to Adam . . .

Gen 3:6-7

⁶AND WHEN THE WOMAN SAW THAT THE TREE WAS GOOD FOR FOOD, AND THAT IT WAS PLEASANT TO THE EYES, AND A TREE TO BE DESIRED TO MAKE ONE WISE, SHE TOOK OF THE FRUIT THEREOF, AND DID EAT, AND GAVE ALSO UNTO HER HUSBAND WITH HER; AND HE DID EAT.

. . . and Adam participated in the *spiritual adultery* of his female side.

Appendix – Verse 1

⁷AND THE EYES OF THEM BOTH WERE OPENED, AND THEY KNEW THAT THEY WERE NAKED; AND THEY SEWED FIG LEAVES TOGETHER, AND MADE THEMSELVES APRONS.

KJV

All of mankind are the residue, the descendants of, the 1st Adam of Creation who married the Snake, the personality of the emotional waters of the abyss, who is appearing today as the carnal mind of fallen mankind.

Gen 4:1

⁴AND ADAM KNEW EVE HIS WIFE; **AND SHE CONCEIVED, AND BARE CAIN,** AND SAID, I HAVE GOTTEN A MAN FROM THE LORD.

KJV

. . . the offspring of the 1st Adam's adulterous wife and the Snake: . . .

Rev 12:9

⁹AND THE GREAT DRAGON WAS CAST OUT, **THAT OLD SERPENT, CALLED THE DEVIL, AND SATAN,** WHICH DECEIVETH THE WHOLE WORLD: HE WAS CAST OUT INTO THE EARTH, AND HIS ANGELS WERE CAST OUT WITH HIM.

KJV

Rev 20:2

²AND HE LAID HOLD ON **THE DRAGON, THAT OLD SERPENT, WHICH IS THE DEVIL, AND SATAN,** AND BOUND HIM A THOUSAND YEARS,

KJV

Abel, The Bisected Adam

The bisected first Adam is half a spiritual male called *Abel*, who is buried under the earthen, animal bodies of mankind, which are formed by Cain.

In the fullness of time, however, God joined himself to Abel, the bisected Adam of creation in the man Jesus of Nazareth, completed him with a new female side, and raised the first Adam of creation from the dead.

Mankind Is Half A Man

The Hebrew word *ish*, **Strong's** #376, translated *man*, means *any male,* or *mortal man.*

Ish is what Adam became after Jehovah bisected him and made a woman out of one of his sides.

Gen 2:21-22

²¹A<small>ND THE</small> L<small>ORD</small> G<small>OD CAUSED A DEEP SLEEP TO FALL UPON</small> A<small>DAM AND HE SLEPT:</small> A*<small>ND HE TOOK ONE OF HIS RIBS</small>*, <small>AND CLOSED UP THE FLESH INSTEAD THEREOF;</small>

²²A*<small>ND THE RIB, WHICH THE</small>* L*<small>ORD</small>* G*<small>OD HAD TAKEN FROM MAN, MADE HE A WOMAN</small>*, <small>AND BROUGHT HER UNTO THE MAN.</small>

²³A<small>ND</small> A<small>DAM SAID,</small> T<small>HIS IS NOW BONE OF MY BONES, AND FLESH OF MY FLESH: SHE SHALL BE CALLED</small> W<small>OMAN, BECAUSE SHE WAS TAKEN OUT OF</small> M<small>AN.</small>

²⁴T<small>HEREFORE SHALL A MAN LEAVE HIS FATHER AND HIS MOTHER, AND SHALL CLEAVE UNTO HIS WIFE: AND THEY SHALL BE ONE FLESH.</small>

Appendix – Verse 1

²⁵AND THEY WERE BOTH NAKED, THE MAN AND HIS WIFE, AND WERE NOT ASHAMED.

KJV

Gen 2:23-25

ALTERNATE TRANSLATION

23a   And Adam said, the Woman shall be called *a spiritual mortal man* (ish), because [she and the Snake

24a   Became one flesh [male organ, and]

23b   Seized [my manhood, and] her bones [the female part], are counterfeits of my spiritual bones, and her flesh [is a counterfeit of] the flesh of my spiritual [male organ],

24b   Wherefore, it is right that I should be loosened from [Jehovah, my] father, and [Binah, my] Mother, and [become Abel], a mortal man (ish) [who] follows [the instructions of Cain], his wife (ishah),

25   And [Cain and Abel] were both naked, and [Cain, who had been] Adam's wife [before she married the Snake], was not ashamed. **(ATB)**

Ish is *half a man*, a mortal man, any old fallen man. But Jesus is not an *ish*. Jesus was an *Adam* in the days of his flesh, and today, in his glorified state, *Jesus is the whole regenerated Righteous Adam.*

Rev 2:8

⁸AND UNTO THE ANGEL OF THE CHURCH IN SMYRNA WRITE; THESE THINGS SAITH *THE FIRST*

AND THE LAST [ADAM], WHICH WAS DEAD, AND IS ALIVE;

KJV

Jesus Is Complete

***Jesus* is *both male and female*.** Righteous Adam is his male side and his purified, perfected humanity is his female side.

Lk 13:32

³²AND HE SAID UNTO THEM, GO YE, AND TELL THAT FOX, BEHOLD, I CAST OUT DEVILS, AND I DO CURES TO DAY AND TO MORROW, AND THE THIRD DAY *I SHALL BE PERFECTED*.

KJV

Jesus Is A Whole Man

Jesus is a whole man, and because he is whole, he can complete all the other *ishes*.

Col 2:10

¹⁰AND *YE ARE COMPLETE IN HIM*, WHICH IS THE HEAD OF ALL PRINCIPALITY AND POWER:

KJV

Righteous Adam Regenerated In Jesus

Righteous Adam was regenerated in Jesus, which made him an Adam, not an *ish*.

This soul within the personality called Jesus of Nazareth (of course he was one with Elijah, and Moses also), had ascended to this high place where they were not destroyed. They became the burning bush which was not destroyed, the 3-fold burning bush (Moses, Elijah and Jesus), that was not destroyed by the fire.

The judgment did not destroy them. There was no sin found in them.

I saw in the night visions, and, behold, one like unto the Son of man came near with the clouds of heaven... Where did they come near to? They came near to the Ancient of days who was sitting on their throne. They *came near to the Ancient of days and they brought him near before him.*

Cain is the offspring of the 1st Adam that died when Jehovah bisected him, to separate him from the Snake who was committing adultery with his female side.

Christ Died For Our Sins

And so the Scripture says,

1 Cor 15:3-4,

³FOR I DELIVERED UNTO YOU FIRST OF ALL THAT WHICH I ALSO RECEIVED, *HOW THAT CHRIST DIED FOR OUR SINS ACCORDING TO THE SCRIPTURES;*

⁴AND THAT HE WAS BURIED, AND THAT HE ROSE AGAIN THE THIRD DAY ACCORDING TO THE SCRIPTURES:

KJV

Paul is saying in Verse 3 that, according to the Scripture, Adam of creation, *the Christ of the Age of Innocence*, died because we, the descendants of his adulterous female side, existed and sinned with the Snake in a previous age.

Buried Under Earthen Bodies

Paul is saying in Verse 4, that the remains of t*he dead Adam of creation, the bisected Christ of the age of innocence*, were buried under the earthen bodies of mortal mankind, and rose again in Jesus of Nazareth by way of a spiritual experience called, ***the third day [of creation]***.

Buried Under The Earth

The regenerated first Adam of creation was raised in a natural, earth man . . .

1 Cor 15:47

⁴⁷THE FIRST MAN IS OF THE EARTH, EARTHY: THE SECOND MAN IS THE LORD FROM HEAVEN.

KJV

The 2nd Adam

. . . who had the potential to mature into a spiritual man, when Christ within him matured into Christ Jesus, ***the second Adam,*** who is

1 Cor 15:47

⁴⁷THE FIRST MAN IS OF THE EARTH, EARTHY: THE SECOND MAN IS ***THE LORD FROM HEAVEN.***

KJV

Jesus of Nazareth became ***Jesus, the Christ, in*** the days of his flesh, because ***the second Adam***, ***the Lord from heaven,*** was appearing within him . . .

Appendix – Verse 1

Mk 5:32-34

ALTERNATE TRANSLATION

³⁴And [Jesus] turned about [toward his spiritual side], to look [for the thief] who had done this thing [with his spiritual sight],

³³But the woman was alarmed [when she realized that Jesus] knew that she had used spiritual power [to steal from God], and went to him, and fell down in front of him, and told him the truth [about what she had done],

³⁴And [**the Second Adam, the Son of God**, and **Jesus of Nazareth, the Son of Man**, agreed to have mercy on the woman, and grant her repentance], **and they said to her [with one voice]**, your belief [in the miracle-working power of God, and the fact that] you were delivered from the plague [proves that you are a] female descendant [of Abraham, so] go in peace and be healthy. **(ATB)**

The Son Of Man

Dan 7:13

¹³I SAW IN THE NIGHT VISIONS, AND, BEHOLD, ONE LIKE *THE SON OF MAN* CAME WITH THE CLOUDS OF HEAVEN, AND CAME TO THE ANCIENT OF DAYS, *AND THEY BROUGHT HIM NEAR BEFORE HIM.*

KJV

Appendix – Verse 1

Jesus, the Son of Man, or the Son of Adam, is a mortal man whose inner, spiritual man was restored to the stature of Righteous Adam of the Age of Innocence.

The Last Adam

. . . and *the Second Adam* became *the last Adam,* when the physical body of Jesus, the Christ, who was spiritual, but still a natural man, was completely transformed and blended together with the second Adam, to became *one glorified man* called *the Lord Jesus Christ*:

Rev 22:13

^{13}I AM ALPHA AND OMEGA, THE BEGINNING AND THE END, THE FIRST AND THE LAST.

KJV

The first Adam of creation in the personality of *the glorified Jesus Christ, the last Adam*, was restored to full power and authority beyond that which Adam had at the beginning.

The glorified Jesus Christ is the visible spiritual garment that clothes the Ancient of Days:

Dan 7:13

^{13}I SAW IN THE NIGHT VISIONS, AND, BEHOLD, ONE LIKE *THE SON OF MAN* CAME WITH THE CLOUDS OF HEAVEN, AND *CAME TO THE ANCIENT OF DAYS*, AND THEY BROUGHT HIM NEAR BEFORE HIM.

KJV

As Joseph Was To Pharaoh

The glorified Jesus, the last Adam, is to Ancient Adam as Joseph was to Pharaoh: Jesus has full power and authority over the creation of God, including ***the authority to forgive sins***, which is the purview of God alone . . .

Mk 2:7

⁷WHY DOTH THIS MAN THUS SPEAK BLASPHEMIES? WHO CAN FORGIVE SINS BUT GOD ONLY?

KJV

Lk 5:21

²¹AND THE SCRIBES AND THE PHARISEES BEGAN TO REASON, SAYING, WHO IS THIS WHICH SPEAKETH BLASPHEMIES? WHO CAN FORGIVE SINS, BUT GOD ALONE?

KJV

. . . but Jesus is not God.

The Ancient of Days

The Ancient of Days is God, and Jesus is his ambassador, just as Pharaoh was a god to the Egyptian people, and Joseph was his Viceroy.

Dan 7:9

⁹I BEHELD TILL THE THRONES WERE CAST DOWN, AND THE ANCIENT OF DAYS DID SIT, ***WHOSE GARMENT WAS WHITE AS SNOW***, AND THE HAIR OF HIS HEAD LIKE THE PURE WOOL: HIS THRONE WAS LIKE THE FIERY FLAME, AND HIS WHEELS AS BURNING FIRE.

KJV

Isa 1:18, which says, ***Come now, and let us reason together, saith the LORD: though your sins be as scarlet, they shall be as white as snow; though they be red like crimson, they shall be as wool.*** Mankind, the fallen earthen Adam, are the garment of Primordial Adam; and we are being purified so that we can abide forever with him.

The first human being to have this experience was Jesus of Nazareth. He was completely divested of his sin nature as indicated by the words ***white as snow*** and he dwells forever with primordial Adam, in the light that no human being can attain unto, the only true immortality.

1 Tim 6:15

¹⁵ WHICH IN HIS TIMES HE SHALL SHEW, WHO IS THE BLESSED AND ONLY POTENTATE, THE KING OF KINGS, AND LORD OF LORDS;

KJV

And the hair of his head like the pure wool, that is interesting. I am not really sure what that verse means but I know that wool is associated with animals, and that God called his people sheep. So that suggests to me that this Scripture is describing the glorified Jesus Christ who took his animal body with him. He purified his animal body and took it with him into the God world of Atzilut. Jesus, the garment of Primordial Adam, was made perfect. All of Jesus, spirit, soul and physical body were blended into a spiritual garment for Primordial Adam that will last forever, and mortal mankind all have the potential to share in Jesus' glorification.

His throne was like the fiery flame, and his wheels as burning fire. His wheels are the sephirot. They are continuously turning; they are multi-dimensional. They were burning, meaning they were purified. Also fire is attributed to Binah which refers to judgment. He is abiding in the eternal fire and he is not burnt. He is now a part of that bush that burns but is not consumed, that bush that Moses saw.

Ex 3:2

²AND THE ANGEL OF THE LORD APPEARED UNTO HIM IN A FLAME OF FIRE OUT OF THE MIDST OF A BUSH: AND HE LOOKED, AND, BEHOLD, THE BUSH BURNED WITH FIRE, AND THE BUSH WAS NOT CONSUMED.

KJV

His throne was like the fiery flame. I would like to review this throne for you. Does anybody remember what his throne is? His throne actually is the location of the male calf, the male calf being the spiritual offspring of a human being, which is the manchild . . .

Rev 12:5

5 AND SHE BROUGHT FORTH A MAN CHILD, WHO WAS TO RULE ALL NATIONS WITH A ROD OF IRON: AND HER CHILD WAS CAUGHT UP UNTO GOD, AND TO HIS THRONE.

KJV

. . . . The throne that Keter, the highest grade of God sits upon, is that male calf. That is as close as he gets to our humanity. That union with the 5 sephirot of the female calf joined with the 1 sephirah of the male calf becomes a throne upon which the highest grade of God sits.

Dan 7:9

⁹I BEHELD TILL THE THRONES WERE CAST DOWN, AND THE ANCIENT OF DAYS DID SIT, WHOSE *GARMENT WAS WHITE AS SNOW*, AND *THE HAIR OF HIS HEAD LIKE THE PURE WOOL*: *HIS THRONE WAS LIKE THE FIERY FLAME*, AND *HIS WHEELS AS BURNING FIRE*.

KJV

White As Snow

His body was purified, *the hairs of his head,* that is his spirit, *were like pure wool,* which means that his animal nature was purified. And *his throne,* the place where he was joined to the world above *was like a fiery flame,* which means he was abiding in the purifying fires of Binah's judgment.

I have not looked at the interlinear text but Daniel 7.13 is talking about the glorified soul of Jesus of Nazareth ascending all the way up to the place where the Ancient of days sits, which is the primordial Adam.

Daniel 7:22: *Until the Ancient of days came, and judgment was given to the saints of the most High; and the time came that the saints possessed the kingdom.*

Until the Ancient of days came... Again I did not look at the interlinear text; I am just doing this off the top of my head. *Until the Ancient of days came* close to man, because the glorified Jesus is bringing the Ancient of days close to humanity. *Until the Ancient of days came* to the rest of the body. Daniel 7:9 described the glorified Jesus, Daniel 7:13 talks about the son of man, not the son of God, but the son of man. This is the resurrected Abel.

Appendix – Verse 1

The difference between the son of man and the son of God is that the son of God is the offspring of the seed of God, but the son of man is the offspring of Adam, not the offspring of the Serpent. The son of man is the resurrected and mature Abel whose name is now Adam, and not the fallen Adam who is the wife and the offspring of the serpent.

As a result of these first 2 verses, the Ancient of days (that is the primordial Adam) came close to humanity, and the judgment was given to the saints. He came close to the rest of the body of Christ and judgment was given to the saints of the most high, that is us. ***And the time came that the saints possessed the kingdom.*** We possess the kingdom on 2 levels. First, the kingdom is this body. This body is the kingdom. I told you earlier that Christ Jesus is the Kingdom inside of us, so the kingdom is inside of us. But the kingdom inside of us will pass away if the body dies. The kingdom was designed to be inside of the body.

The time came that the saints possessed the kingdom. We are the saints of God, the personalities' humanity is the saints, and we have to possess the kingdom inside of us. When we possess the kingdom inside of us, our bodies do not die. If our bodies die, the manifestation of the kingdom inside of us departs from the earth, and takes up residence somewhere else, however that works.

For us to die, it has to mean that Christ Jesus in us was not harvested. This is exactly what I was telling you about. Christ Jesus that is not harvested, who is dependent for his existence on the earth, if the earth dies, if we do not possess the kingdom, then it means that he was never permanently attached to the male Adam, and then when we die, he dies. We have to possess the kingdom inside of ourselves first. Does anybody not understand that? Does anybody need me to say that again?

There is a kingdom inside of us. We have the ability today, for 2000 years now it has been possible for a human being to lay hold of that kingdom and join to it so completely, to work

Appendix – Verse 1

with it to join to the male Adam above that we should inherit eternal life. It has been possible for 2000 years but it has not happened since then. It happened to the apostles.

I believe it happened to the apostles because Paul said in the Book of Hebrews that the kingdom of God is built upon the foundation of the apostles and the prophets, Jesus Christ being the chief corner stone. They are a part of that burning bush that abides in the high realms of the spirit without being consumed.

APPENDIX - Verse 2

Reference Scriptures for Verse 2

R-1 Mal 1:2-3
R-2 Ex 20:1-17

Mal 1:2-3

²I HAVE LOVED YOU, SAITH THE LORD. YET YE SAY, WHEREIN HAST THOU LOVED US? WAS NOT ESAU JACOB'S BROTHER? SAITH THE LORD : YET I LOVED JACOB,

³AND I HATED ESAU, AND LAID HIS MOUNTAINS AND HIS HERITAGE WASTE FOR THE DRAGONS OF THE WILDERNESS.

KJV

Ex 20:1-17

¹AND GOD SPAKE ALL THESE WORDS, SAYING,

²I AM THE LORD THY GOD, WHICH HAVE BROUGHT THEE OUT OF THE LAND OF EGYPT, OUT OF THE HOUSE OF BONDAGE.

³THOU SHALT HAVE NO OTHER GODS BEFORE ME.

⁴THOU SHALT NOT MAKE UNTO THEE ANY GRAVEN IMAGE, OR ANY LIKENESS OF ANY THING THAT IS IN HEAVEN ABOVE, OR THAT IS IN THE EARTH BENEATH, OR THAT IS IN THE WATER UNDER THE EARTH:

Appendix – Verse 2

⁵THOU SHALT NOT BOW DOWN THYSELF TO THEM, NOR SERVE THEM: FOR I THE LORD THY GOD AM A JEALOUS GOD, VISITING THE INIQUITY OF THE FATHERS UPON THE CHILDREN UNTO THE THIRD AND FOURTH GENERATION OF THEM THAT HATE ME;

⁶AND SHEWING MERCY UNTO THOUSANDS OF THEM THAT LOVE ME, AND KEEP MY COMMANDMENTS.

⁷THOU SHALT NOT TAKE THE NAME OF THE LORD THY GOD IN VAIN; FOR THE LORD WILL NOT HOLD HIM GUILTLESS THAT TAKETH HIS NAME IN VAIN.

⁸REMEMBER THE SABBATH DAY, TO KEEP IT HOLY.

⁹SIX DAYS SHALT THOU LABOUR, AND DO ALL THY WORK:

¹⁰BUT THE SEVENTH DAY IS THE SABBATH OF THE LORD THY GOD: IN IT THOU SHALT NOT DO ANY WORK, THOU, NOR THY SON, NOR THY DAUGHTER, THY MANSERVANT, NOR THY MAIDSERVANT, NOR THY CATTLE, NOR THY STRANGER THAT IS WITHIN THY GATES:

¹¹FOR IN SIX DAYS THE LORD MADE HEAVEN AND EARTH, THE SEA, AND ALL THAT IN THEM IS, AND RESTED THE SEVENTH DAY: WHEREFORE THE LORD BLESSED THE SABBATH DAY, AND HALLOWED IT.

¹²HONOUR THY FATHER AND THY MOTHER: THAT THY DAYS MAY BE LONG UPON THE LAND WHICH THE LORD THY GOD GIVETH THEE.

Appendix – Verse 2

¹³Thou shalt not kill.

¹⁴Thou shalt not commit adultery.

¹⁵Thou shalt not steal.

¹⁶Thou shalt not bear false witness against thy neighbour.

¹⁷Thou shalt not covet thy neighbour's house, thou shalt not covet thy neighbour's wife, nor his manservant, nor his maidservant, nor his ox, nor his ass, nor any thing that is thy neighbour's.

KJV

APPENDIX – Verse 3

Reference Scriptures for Verse 3

^R Rev 12:5

Rev 12:5

⁵AND SHE BROUGHT FORTH A MAN CHILD, WHO WAS TO RULE ALL NATIONS WITH A ROD OF IRON: AND HER CHILD WAS CAUGHT UP UNTO GOD, AND TO HIS THRONE.

KJV

APPENDIX – Verse 4

Reference Scriptures for Verse 4

[R] Heb 12:2

Heb 12:2

²L͟ooking unto Jesus the author and finisher of our faith; who for the joy that was set before him endured the cross, despising the shame, and is set down at the right hand of the throne of God.

KJV

APPENDIX – Verse 5

Reference Scriptures for Verse 5

[R] Rom 11:20

Rom 11:20

[20] WELL; BECAUSE OF UNBELIEF THEY WERE BROKEN OFF, AND THOU STANDEST BY FAITH. BE NOT HIGHMINDED, BUT FEAR:

KJV

APPENDIX – Verse 6

Reference Scriptures for Verse 6

[R-1] Lk 3:23
[R-2] Gal 3:16
[R-3] Jn 1:17

Lk 3:2

²³AND JESUS HIMSELF BEGAN TO BE ABOUT THIRTY YEARS OF AGE, BEING (AS WAS SUPPOSED) THE SON OF JOSEPH, WHICH WAS THE SON OF HELI,

KJV

Gal 3:16

¹⁶NOW TO ABRAHAM AND HIS SEED WERE THE PROMISES MADE. HE SAITH NOT, AND TO SEEDS, AS OF MANY; BUT AS OF ONE, AND TO THY SEED, WHICH IS CHRIST.

KJV

Jn 1:17

¹⁷FOR THE LAW WAS GIVEN BY MOSES, BUT GRACE AND TRUTH CAME BY JESUS CHRIST.

KJV

Footnotes for Verse 6

Footnote #3

Mankind Is Spiritually Female

How can the female seed of a human male produce a male, physical child? The answer is that all of humanity is spiritually female in relation to God, so even though Joseph's seed produced a physical male, from the spiritual point of view, the seed that produced the male, physical body of Jesus, was spiritually female.

Footnote #4

Joseph Is Jesus' Flesh Father
As Supposed

Lk 3:23

²³AND JESUS HIMSELF BEGAN TO BE ABOUT THIRTY YEARS OF AGE, BEING (*AS WAS SUPPOSED*) THE SON OF JOSEPH, WHICH WAS THE SON OF HELI,

KJV

The English words, *as supposed*, in the King James Translation of Lk 3:23, are a translation of two Greek words which mean, *according to the commonly accepted custom.*

Lk 3:23

²³AND JESUS HIMSELF BEGAN TO BE ABOUT THIRTY YEARS OF AGE, *BEING (AS WAS SUPPOSED)* THE SON OF JOSEPH, WHICH WAS THE SON OF HELI,

KJV

. . . *being (as was supposed) the son of Joseph,* means that Jesus lived as a member of the local community and was known as the son of Joseph, the father of his flesh, rather than as the Son of his spiritual Father, even though he was an incarnation of a high principality in the Kingdom of God.

Matt 2:2

² SAYING, WHERE IS HE THAT IS BORN KING OF THE JEWS? FOR *WE HAVE SEEN HIS STAR IN THE EAST, AND ARE COME TO WORSHIP HIM.*

KJV

Luke 3:23, when understood correctly, clearly indicates that Joseph provided the physical male seed that produced Jesus of Nazareth. But even more convincing than that, is the fact that, according to Matthew, Mary descends from David's son, Nathan (Lk 3:31), and not from Solomon, the prophesied progenitor of Messiah.

Lk 3:31

³¹ WHICH WAS THE SON OF MELEA, WHICH WAS THE SON OF MENAN, WHICH WAS THE SON OF MATTATHA, WHICH WAS THE SON OF NATHAN, WHICH WAS THE SON OF DAVID,

KJV

Found With Child

Matt 1:18

¹⁸NOW THE BIRTH OF JESUS CHRIST WAS ON THIS WISE: WHEN AS HIS MOTHER MARY WAS ESPOUSED TO JOSEPH, *BEFORE THEY CAME TOGETHER, SHE WAS FOUND WITH CHILD OF THE HOLY GHOST.*

KJV

The English words, **with child**, are a translation of three Greek words which mean, *in*, *belly or womb*, and *possessed*, respectively.

The whole phrase is: *before they came together in the womb possessed of the Holy Ghost*. There is no Greek word that means, *child*.

The correct translation is: *before they came together, the Holy Ghost was [already] possessing Mary's womb*. The suggestion is that the Holy Spirit was possessing Mary's womb to control which egg and sperm would be involved in the conception of Jesus, before Mary and Joseph ever came together.

The Fetal Jesus

Heb 2:16

¹⁶FOR VERILY HE TOOK NOT ON HIM THE NATURE OF ANGELS; BUT HE TOOK ON HIM THE SEED OF ABRAHAM.

KJV

Appendix – Verse 6

Heb 2:16
ALTERNATE TRANSLATION

2:16 Because, truly, the angel did not seize [Jesus for himself], but [the Holy Spirit] seized [the fetal Jesus in Mary's womb to be a vessel for] Abraham's seed. **(ATB)**

A Public Example

Matt 1:19

¹⁹THEN JOSEPH HER HUSBAND, BEING A JUST MAN, AND *NOT WILLING TO MAKE HER A PUBLICK EXAMPLE*, WAS MINDED TO PUT HER AWAY PRIVILY.

KJV

. . . Joseph was concerned that Mary would be mocked because she was saying that Gabriel had visited her, etc. and considered divorcing her.

Joseph's Lineage

King Jechonais

Jesus is a descendant of King Jechonias, the last of the Judean kings, through Joseph.

Matt 1:11-16

¹²AND AFTER THEY WERE BROUGHT TO BABYLON, *JECHONIAS BEGAT* SALATHIEL; AND SALATHIEL BEGAT ZOROBABEL;

Appendix – Verse 6

¹³AND ZOROBABEL BEGAT ABIUD; AND ABIUD BEGAT ELIAKIM; AND ELIAKIM BEGAT AZOR;

¹⁴AND AZOR BEGAT SADOC; AND SADOC BEGAT ACHIM; AND ACHIM BEGAT ELIUD;

¹⁵AND ELIUD BEGAT ELEAZAR; AND ELEAZAR BEGAT MATTHAN; AND MATTHAN BEGAT JACOB;

¹⁶*AND JACOB BEGAT JOSEPH THE HUSBAND OF MARY, OF WHOM WAS BORN JESUS, WHO IS CALLED CHRIST.*

KJV

Write This Man Childless

Some argue that Joseph's lineage cannot produce Messiah, because Jeremiah cursed King Jechonias (Jer 22:30), saying that no descendant of his would ever sit on the throne of Judah.

Jeremiah 22:30 was an extremely difficult verse to translate. Christ Jesus within me was not able to translate this verse by himself. The Lord Jesus had to descend into my spiritual universe to assist him. The proof of this is that I rendered this Alternate Translation last night, but could not repeat how I did it this morning. I had to rethink the whole translation this morning to prepare myself to teach, and could not have done it if I did not have the text from last night.

One of my translating practices is to make sure that the same amount of negatives in the original text appear in my translation, not one more nor one less. The King James translation shows three negatives for this verse, but the Interlinear Text shows that the words translated, ***shall not*** *prosper*, appear twice, which accounts for the fourth negative: not prosper, no man, no more (anymore), not prosper.

Jer 22:28-30

²⁸IS *THIS MAN CONIAH* A DESPISED BROKEN IDOL? IS HE A VESSEL WHEREIN IS NO PLEASURE? WHEREFORE ARE THEY CAST OUT, HE AND HIS SEED, AND ARE CAST INTO A LAND WHICH THEY KNOW NOT?

²⁹O EARTH, EARTH, EARTH, HEAR THE WORD OF THE LORD.

³⁰THUS SAITH THE LORD, *WRITE YE THIS MAN CHILDLESS*, A MAN THAT SHALL NOT PROSPER IN HIS DAYS: *FOR NO MAN OF HIS SEED SHALL PROSPER, SITTING UPON THE THRONE OF DAVID, AND RULING ANY MORE IN JUDAH.*

KJV

Coniah is another spelling of *Jechonias*:

JEHOIACHIN

[juh HOI uh kin] (the Lord establishes) - the son and successor of Jehoiakim as king of Judah, about 598 or 597 B.C. (2 Chron 36:8-9; Ez 1:2).

Jehoiachin is also called Jeconiah (1 Chron 3:16-17) ***and Coniah*** (Jer 22:24). In the New Testament he is listed by Matthew as an ancestor of Jesus (Matt 1:11-12).

(from Nelson's Illustrated Bible Dictionary, Copyright © 1986, Thomas Nelson Publishers)

Appendix – Verse 6

Jer 22:30
Alternate Translation Work Up

Thus says Jehovah, Write this mortal man (***Strong's*** #376), [Jechonias] shall be childless: Neither [Righteous Adam], the [spiritual] warrior (man=***Strong's*** 1397) [that defends Israel], nor his descendant, shall incarnate in his lifetime, and no mortal man (***Strong's*** #376) shall incarnate that will sit on the throne of David, continuing to rule in Judah.

Thus says Jehovah, [Ancient Adam], the [spiritual] warrior (man) [that defends Israel], shall not push forth into [King Jechoniah], this mortal man [who is his] mate, [during] the days [that] he sits on the throne of David, nor shall [Righteous Adam] push forth and engrave (write) [King Jechoniah with the nature of Ancient Adam], nor shall [Ancient Adam's male] heir ᴿ be born (childless) in [King Jechoniah], and no mortal man shall continue to rule in Judah [after King Jechoniah is removed from the throne].

Rev 12:5

⁵AND SHE BROUGHT FORTH A MAN CHILD, WHO WAS TO RULE ALL NATIONS WITH A ROD OF IRON: AND HER CHILD WAS CAUGHT UP UNTO GOD, AND TO HIS THRONE.

KJV

Jer 22:29-30
ALTERNATE TRANSLATION

30a   Thus says Jehovah to [King Jechoniah], this mortal man [who is his] mate, [during] the days [that] he sits on the throne of David,

29a   Hear the word of the Lord,

30b [Ancient Adam], the [spiritual] warrior [that defends Israel], shall not push forth [his seed] into [the human spirit of your] [R-1]

29b Earth[en soul, and]

30c [Righteous Adam] shall not push forth into [your]

29c Earth[en soul]

30d To engrave [it with the nature of Ancient Adam],[R-2] nor shall [Ancient Adam's male] heir[R3] be born in [your]

29d Earth[en body, and]

30e No mortal man shall continue to rule in Judah [after you depart from the throne]. **(ATB)**

[R-1] This is the 30-fold anointing, where the sown seed of the Lord pierces Abel, the spiritual root of Righteous Adam in the hearer of the Word.*

[R-2] This is the 60-fold anointing, where Abel, the spiritual root of Righteous Adam, begins to increase into the six Sefirot of Christ Jesus.*

[R-3] This is the 100-fold anointing, which are the 10 Sefirot of the regenerated, completed Righteous Adam in the hearer of the Word.*

*/

Message #818.11, Degrees of Salvation
Matt 13:8 and 23

Interspersed

ALTERNATE TRANSLATION

8 and 23 But the seed [of the Shekinah], the Rock [that accompanied the Hebrew children when they left Egypt], that fell down upon the good ground [of the students who pursued the spiritual life], that extended into some of [the students whose lifestyle] was virtuous, heard the Word [about the Kingdom of God], and understood it, and become fertile, and brought forth fruit [in three degrees]:

An **hundred**fold, [which is] Binah, [the Mother, who is] Understanding,

The six Sefirot of [Christ Jesus, the Son of] God, [the ten Sub-Sefirot of which are] **sixty**, [who is], indeed, [the Spirit of] Truth, and

The ten Sub-Sefirot of [Binah], the third Sefirah [of the higher world, which are] **thirty**, [which descend into] Malchut, the other [female Sefirah of the higher world, as the seed that imposes the DNA of the higher world upon the lower world] **(ATB)**

British Israel

It is important to note at this point, that the above translation of Jeremiah 22:30 contradicts the teachings of Mr. J. H. Allen, a strong proponent of *the Doctrine of British Israel,* which teaches that a physical heir of David will sit as King on a physical throne forever. Mr. Allen believes that England is that throne, and that the English monarch sitting on the throne when Messiah appears, will abdicate in favor of Messiah.

As far as I can see, Mr. Allen bases his theory primarily upon the following two Scriptures:

Appendix – Verse 6

Gen 49:10

¹⁰THE SCEPTRE SHALL NOT DEPART FROM JUDAH, NOR A LAWGIVER FROM BETWEEN HIS FEET, UNTIL SHILOH COME; AND UNTO HIM SHALL THE GATHERING OF THE PEOPLE BE.

KJV

Gen 49:10

Alternate Translation Work Up

Not depart the male authority to rule (scepter) from Judah or (until) the one who engraves in between the female foot until comes Shilo belongs to the obedience of the people.

Gen 49:10

ALTERNATE TRANSLATION

49:10 [Ancient Adam's] male authority to rule shall not depart from Judah, nor [Righteous Adam], the one who engraves [Cain with the nature of God, who is] in between [ancient Adam and Abel], the female foot [of righteous Adam in the earth of mankind], until Shilo comes, and the people who belong to him shall obey him. **(ATB)**

When Messiah comes, the kingdom of God will replace the Judean monarchal system, and ruling authority will become internalized in the individual.

Appendix – Verse 6

1 Ki 8:25

²⁵THEREFORE NOW, LORD GOD OF ISRAEL, KEEP WITH THY SERVANT DAVID MY FATHER THAT THOU PROMISEDST HIM, SAYING, THERE SHALL NOT FAIL THEE A MAN IN MY SIGHT TO SIT ON THE THRONE OF ISRAEL; SO THAT THY CHILDREN TAKE HEED TO THEIR WAY, THAT THEY WALK BEFORE ME AS THOU HAST WALKED BEFORE ME.

KJV

1 Kings 8:25

Alternate Translation Work Up

At this time (therefore now) Jehovah God Israel keep servant David father promise belong to (him) saying not cut/covenant (fail) belong to personality (in my sight) sit down on throne Israel although not (so that) protect (take heed) children course of life (way) walk personality (before me) self (as) carry personality (before me)

At this time (therefore now) Jehovah God Israel protect servant David father speak belong to saying not cut/covenant belong to personality sit down on throne Israel although not protect children course of life walk personality self carry personality

Appendix – Verse 6

1 Ki 8:25

ALTERNATE TRANSLATION

25   At this time, may Jehovah, the God Israel, keep his promise to his servant, David, my father, [when] he said [that], He will not cut off the personality that belongs to the mortal man that is married to the throne of Israel above, except to preserve the personality of the children as they pass through this dangerous life, like the [other, first] personality of himself, walked. **(ATB)**

1st Kings 8:25 is speaking about the immortality of the Israelites. Jehovah promised immortality in the flesh for every man who is attached to the throne of God from above, that is, the spiritual throne in Beriah, with the exception of the man who is Messiah, who is destined to be cut off so that the other children can pass through this dangerous life safely in the same manner that he did.

These verses have nothing to do with a physical kingdom, sitting on a physical throne continuously from the time of the monarchial Judean Kings, until the coming of Messiah. Mr. JH Allen, the author of Judah's Scepter and Joseph's Birthright, has based a whole doctrine, the doctrine of British Israel, on the King James translation of an enigmatic, very difficult to translate, Scripture.

I still believe a lot of things that he says such as King Zedekiah's daughters arriving in Ireland and marrying a Prince of Zereh, Judah's true firstborn by virtue of the red string on his wrist. I believe all of the witnesses of Joseph's coat of many colors in Scotland, and the Cohan's in Ireland, etc. and I believe that the monarchies of England's claim to descend from Judah, because it is probably true. But none of this leads me to the conclusion that this is the fulfillment of prophecies that Jehovah said that a man will always be on the throne, which then leads to the conclusion that the British monarchy will turn over the throne to Messiah when he comes.

Conclusion
To The Study Of Joseph Is Jesus' Flesh Father:

Joseph's Lineage Qualifies Jesus to Be Messiah

Jesus, the son of Joseph, a descendant of King Jechonias, is **NOT** excluded from being Messiah because of Jeremiahs curse, which says that an *ish*, a mortal man who is not possessed by Righteous Adam, cannot continue the rule of the Davidic Dynasty.

Jehovah told Jeremiah to pronounce the curse, and only Jehovah can regenerate Adam in the man that he chooses to resurrect the Davidic Dynasty.

Any mortal man that Jehovah might have regenerated Righteous Adam in, even a son of Jechonias, would have survived Jeremiah's curse.

APPENDIX – Verse 7

Reference Scriptures for Verse 7

[R-1] Heb 4:14
[R-2] Pro 9:1
[R-3] Rev 19:13
[R-4] Pro 24:3
[R-5] Dan 7:9
[R-6] Acts 17:28

Heb 4:14

¹⁴SEEING THEN THAT WE HAVE A GREAT HIGH PRIEST, THAT IS PASSED INTO THE HEAVENS, JESUS THE SON OF GOD, LET US HOLD FAST OUR PROFESSION.

KJV

Prov 9:1

¹WISDOM HATH BUILDED HER HOUSE, SHE HATH HEWN OUT HER SEVEN PILLARS:

KJV

Rev 19:13

¹³AND HE WAS CLOTHED WITH A VESTURE DIPPED IN BLOOD: AND HIS NAME IS CALLED THE WORD OF GOD.

KJV

Appendix – Verse 7

Prov 24:3

³THROUGH WISDOM IS AN HOUSE BUILDED; AND BY UNDERSTANDING IT IS ESTABLISHED:

KJV

Dan 7:9

⁹I BEHELD TILL THE THRONES WERE CAST DOWN, AND THE ANCIENT OF DAYS DID SIT, WHOSE GARMENT WAS WHITE AS SNOW, AND THE HAIR OF HIS HEAD LIKE THE PURE WOOL: HIS THRONE WAS LIKE THE FIERY FLAME, AND HIS WHEELS AS BURNING FIRE.

KJV

Acts 17:28

²⁸FOR IN HIM WE LIVE, AND MOVE, AND HAVE OUR BEING; AS CERTAIN ALSO OF YOUR OWN POETS HAVE SAID, FOR WE ARE ALSO HIS OFFSPRING.

KJV

Appendix – Verse 7

Footnotes for Verse 7

Footnote #5

Jesus Is The Son Of God In Heaven
The First Witness

The Father is the personality associated with the Sefirah, ***Chochmah***, and his attribute is ***Wisdom***:

Prov 9:1

¹WISDOM HATH BUILDED HER HOUSE, SHE HATH HEWN OUT HER SEVEN PILLARS:

KJV

Wisdom

Wisdom carves seven Sefirot out of the Rock (the Shekinah) and they become the spiritual foundation of the man who is coming into existence:

Ex 33:22

²²AND IT SHALL COME TO PASS, WHILE MY GLORY PASSETH BY, THAT I WILL PUT THEE IN *A CLIFT OF THE ROCK*, AND WILL COVER THEE WITH MY HAND WHILE I PASS BY:

KJV

Dan 2:45

⁴⁵FORASMUCH AS THOU SAWEST THAT *THE STONE WAS CUT OUT OF THE MOUNTAIN WITHOUT*

***HANDS*,** AND THAT IT BRAKE IN PIECES THE IRON, THE BRASS, THE CLAY, THE SILVER, AND THE GOLD; THE GREAT GOD HATH MADE KNOWN TO THE KING WHAT SHALL COME TO PASS HEREAFTER: AND THE DREAM IS CERTAIN, AND THE INTERPRETATION THEREOF SURE.

KJV

1 Cor 10:4

⁴AND DID ALL DRINK THE SAME SPIRITUAL DRINK: FOR THEY DRANK OF **THAT SPIRITUAL ROCK** THAT FOLLOWED THEM: **AND THAT ROCK WAS CHRIST**.

KJV

The Anointing

Christ is the Greek word that means ***anointed, the anointed of God***. Paul most likely uses the word ***Christ,*** rather than ***the Shekinah***, because the Greek Christians either were not familiar with the word ***Shekinah***, or were more comfortable with the Greek word, ***Christ***.

A Garment For Ancient Adam

In any event, some think, albeit incorrectly, that the man, Jesus, appeared in other, pre-incarnate forms, from time to time, but this is not true. Jesus is the garment that clothes the Shekinah who accompanied Israel in the wilderness, and after that appeared from behind Jesus of Nazareth:

Appendix – Verse 7

Song 2:9

⁹**MY BELOVED** IS LIKE A ROE OR A YOUNG HART: BEHOLD, HE **STANDETH BEHIND OUR WALL, HE LOOKETH FORTH AT THE WINDOWS,** SHEWING HIMSELF THROUGH THE LATTICE. …

KJV

…and they become the spiritual foundation of the man who is coming into existence (Pro 9:1).

The Father is a witness that Jesus is the Son of God, because it was his spiritual seed that engraved Jesus' spiritual foundation with Jehovah's nature.

Footnote #6

Jesus Is The Son Of God

The Second Witness

The Word of God is *Ancient Adam*. The Kabbalists call him *Adam Kadmon, Primordial human*.

Ancient Adam, the Word of God, is the Sefirah, *Keter*, and the personality associated with the Keter is *the Grandfather*.

Grandfather engraves the first three Sefirot of the lower world (Keter, Chochmah, Binah) with the spiritual DNA from the world above.

Ancient Adam, the Word of God. is a witness that Jesus is the Son of God, because *Jesus, the Son of Man*, approached him and was not destroyed:

Dan 7:13

¹³I SAW IN THE NIGHT VISIONS, AND, BEHOLD, ONE LIKE *THE SON OF MAN CAME* WITH THE CLOUDS OF HEAVEN, **AND CAME TO THE ANCIENT OF DAYS, AND THEY BROUGHT HIM NEAR BEFORE HIM.**

KJV

On the contrary, Jesus became the clothing of Ancient Adam and received dominion, and glory, and a kingdom . . .

Dan 7:14

¹⁴AND THERE WAS GIVEN HIM **DOMINION, AND GLORY, AND A KINGDOM, THAT ALL PEOPLE, NATIONS, AND LANGUAGES, SHOULD SERVE HIM:** HIS DOMINION IS AN EVERLASTING DOMINION, WHICH SHALL NOT PASS AWAY, AND HIS KINGDOM THAT WHICH SHALL NOT BE DESTROYED.

KJV

Footnote #7

Jesus Is The Son Of God

The Third Witness

The Holy Spirit that John references here comes from the third Sefirah called Binah. Her attribute is ***Understanding*** and her personality is ***Mother***. The Kabbalists call her ***the Supernal Mother*** because she comes from the God world of Atzilut.

The Holy Spirit in the Church is not the Supernal Mother who is associated with the grade of Binah. The Holy Spirit in the Church pours out of the 10th Sefirah, which is Malchut. Her personality is ***the Daughter*** of the Supernal Mother, and her attribute is female. This means that she has no attribute of her own, but has the attributes of the other nine Sefirot, all of which compete to be revealed through her.

The Supernal Mother is a witness that Jesus is the Son of God because she sent Gabriel to explain Jesus's birth to Mary, who explained it to Jesus:

Lk 1:26-33

[26] AND IN THE SIXTH MONTH THE ANGEL GABRIEL WAS SENT FROM GOD UNTO A CITY OF GALILEE, NAMED NAZARETH,

[27] TO A VIRGIN ESPOUSED TO A MAN WHOSE NAME WAS JOSEPH, OF THE HOUSE OF DAVID; AND THE VIRGIN'S NAME WAS MARY.

[28] AND THE ANGEL CAME IN UNTO HER, AND SAID, HAIL, THOU THAT ART HIGHLY FAVOURED, THE LORD IS WITH THEE: BLESSED ART THOU AMONG WOMEN.

[29] AND WHEN SHE SAW HIM, SHE WAS TROUBLED AT HIS SAYING, AND CAST IN HER MIND WHAT MANNER OF SALUTATION THIS SHOULD BE.

[30] AND THE ANGEL SAID UNTO HER, FEAR NOT, MARY: FOR THOU HAST FOUND FAVOUR WITH GOD.

[31] AND, BEHOLD, THOU SHALT CONCEIVE IN THY WOMB, AND BRING FORTH A SON, AND SHALT CALL HIS NAME JESUS.

[32] HE SHALL BE GREAT, AND SHALL BE CALLED THE SON OF THE HIGHEST: AND THE LORD GOD SHALL GIVE UNTO HIM THE THRONE OF HIS FATHER DAVID:

Appendix – Verse 7

³³AND HE SHALL REIGN OVER THE HOUSE OF JACOB FOR EVER; AND OF HIS KINGDOM THERE SHALL BE NO END.

KJV

APPENDIX – Verse 8

Reference Scriptures for Verse 8

[R-1] Rom 8:15
Gal 4:6
[R-2] Lk 3:23
[R-3] Gal 3:16
[R-4] 1 Tim 2:5

Rom 8:15

¹⁵FOR YE HAVE NOT RECEIVED THE SPIRIT OF BONDAGE AGAIN TO FEAR; BUT YE HAVE RECEIVED THE SPIRIT OF ADOPTION, WHEREBY WE CRY, ABBA, FATHER.

KJV

Gal 4:6

⁶AND BECAUSE YE ARE SONS, GOD HATH SENT FORTH THE SPIRIT OF HIS SON INTO YOUR HEARTS, CRYING, ABBA, FATHER.

KJV

Lk 3:23

²³AND JESUS HIMSELF BEGAN TO BE ABOUT THIRTY YEARS OF AGE, BEING (AS WAS SUPPOSED) THE SON OF JOSEPH, WHICH WAS THE SON OF HELI,

KJV

Gal 3:16

¹⁶Now to Abraham and his seed were the promises made. He saith not, And to seeds, as of many; but as of one, And to thy seed, which is Christ.

KJV

1 Tim 2:5

⁵For there is one God, and one mediator between God and men, the man Christ Jesus;

KJV

Footnotes for Verse 8

Footnote #8

The Human Spirit In The Earth

The First Witness

The human spirit in a man is the Shekinah in captivity.

The human spirit is a witness that Jesus is the Son of God because the spiritual seed of the Father grafted to it, proving that the two are genetically compatible:

Jas 1:21

²¹Wherefore lay apart all filthiness and superfluity of naughtiness, and receive with meekness ***the engrafted word,*** which is able to save your souls.

KJV

Footnote #9

Joseph's Seed

The Second Witness

The human spirit and the female side of the spiritual seed of the Father are the Shekinah.

Joseph is a descendant of David, a descendant of Jacob who received the seed of God's spiritual intelligence.

Joseph's seed is a witness that Jesus is the Son of God, because the Shekinah within Jesus recognized Jacob's seed within Joseph, and acknowledged that ***Jesus is the land that Jehovah promised Jacob's seed***:

Gen 28:10-14

¹⁰AND JACOB WENT OUT FROM BEER-SHEBA, AND WENT TOWARD HARAN.

¹¹AND HE LIGHTED UPON A CERTAIN PLACE, AND TARRIED THERE ALL NIGHT, BECAUSE THE SUN WAS SET; AND HE TOOK OF THE STONES OF THAT PLACE, AND PUT THEM FOR HIS PILLOWS, AND LAY DOWN IN THAT PLACE TO SLEEP.

¹²AND HE DREAMED, AND BEHOLD A LADDER SET UP ON THE EARTH, AND THE TOP OF IT REACHED TO HEAVEN: AND BEHOLD THE ANGELS OF GOD ASCENDING AND DESCENDING ON IT.

¹³AND, BEHOLD, THE LORD STOOD ABOVE IT, AND SAID, I AM THE LORD GOD OF ABRAHAM THY FATHER, AND THE GOD OF ISAAC: **THE LAND WHEREON THOU LIEST, TO THEE WILL I GIVE IT, AND TO THY SEED**;

¹⁴AND THY SEED SHALL BE AS THE DUST OF THE EARTH, AND THOU SHALT SPREAD ABROAD TO THE WEST, AND TO THE EAST, AND TO THE NORTH,

AND TO THE SOUTH: AND IN THEE AND IN THY SEED SHALL ALL THE FAMILIES OF THE EARTH BE BLESSED.

KJV

Footnote #10

Abraham's Seed Is Christ

The Third Witness

Gal 3:16

¹⁶NOW TO ABRAHAM AND HIS SEED WERE THE PROMISES MADE. HE SAITH NOT, AND TO SEEDS, AS OF MANY; BUT AS OF ONE, AND TO THY SEED, WHICH IS CHRIST.

KJV

Christ in Jesus is a witness that Jesus is the Son of God, because Christ rose from the dead in the man, Jesus:

1 Cor 15:3-4

³FOR I DELIVERED UNTO YOU FIRST OF ALL THAT WHICH I ALSO RECEIVED, HOW THAT CHRIST DIED FOR OUR SINS ACCORDING TO THE SCRIPTURES;

⁴AND THAT HE WAS BURIED, AND THAT HE ROSE AGAIN THE THIRD DAY ACCORDING TO THE SCRIPTURES:

KJV

APPENDIX – Verse 9

Reference Scriptures for Verse 9

[R-1] Ex 7:14-18
[R-2] Col 2:10

Ex 7:14-18

¹⁴AND THE LORD SAID UNTO MOSES, PHARAOH'S HEART IS HARDENED, HE REFUSETH TO LET THE PEOPLE GO.

¹⁵GET THEE UNTO PHARAOH IN THE MORNING; LO, HE GOETH OUT UNTO THE WATER; AND THOU SHALT STAND BY THE RIVER'S BRINK AGAINST HE COME; AND THE ROD WHICH WAS TURNED TO A SERPENT SHALT THOU TAKE IN THINE HAND.

¹⁶AND THOU SHALT SAY UNTO HIM, THE LORD GOD OF THE HEBREWS HATH SENT ME UNTO THEE, SAYING, LET MY PEOPLE GO, THAT THEY MAY SERVE ME IN THE WILDERNESS: AND, BEHOLD, HITHERTO THOU WOULDEST NOT HEAR.

¹⁷THUS SAITH THE LORD, IN THIS THOU SHALT KNOW THAT I AM THE LORD : BEHOLD, I WILL SMITE WITH THE ROD THAT IS IN MINE HAND UPON THE WATERS WHICH ARE IN THE RIVER, AND THEY SHALL BE TURNED TO BLOOD.

¹⁸AND THE FISH THAT IS IN THE RIVER SHALL DIE, AND THE RIVER SHALL STINK; AND THE EGYPTIANS SHALL LOTHE TO DRINK OF THE WATER OF THE RIVER.

KJV

Appendix – Verse 9

Col 2:10

¹⁰AND YE ARE COMPLETE IN HIM, WHICH IS THE HEAD OF ALL PRINCIPALITY AND POWER:

KJV

APPENDIX – Verse 10

Reference Scriptures for Verse 10

[R] 1 Thess. 2:11

1 Thess 2:11

[11]AS YE KNOW HOW WE EXHORTED AND COMFORTED AND CHARGED EVERY ONE OF YOU, AS A FATHER DOTH HIS CHILDREN,

KJV

APPENDIX – Verse 11

Reference Scriptures for Verse 11

[R-1] Jn 17:3
[R-2] Jn 6:54

Jn 17:3

³AND THIS IS LIFE ETERNAL, THAT THEY MIGHT KNOW THEE THE ONLY TRUE GOD, AND JESUS CHRIST, WHOM THOU HAST SENT.

KJV

Jn 6:54

⁵⁴WHOSO EATETH MY FLESH, AND DRINKETH MY BLOOD, HATH ETERNAL LIFE; AND I WILL RAISE HIM UP AT THE LAST DAY.

KJV

APPENDIX – Verse 12

Reference Scriptures for Verse 12

[R-1] Col 1:27
[R-2] Jn 10:28
Rom 6:23

Col 1:27

²⁷TO WHOM GOD WOULD MAKE KNOWN WHAT IS THE RICHES OF THE GLORY OF THIS MYSTERY AMONG THE GENTILES; WHICH IS CHRIST IN YOU, THE HOPE OF GLORY:

KJV

Jn 10:28

²⁸AND I GIVE UNTO THEM ETERNAL LIFE; AND THEY SHALL NEVER PERISH, NEITHER SHALL ANY MAN PLUCK THEM OUT OF MY HAND.

KJV

Rom 6:23

²³FOR THE WAGES OF SIN IS DEATH; BUT THE GIFT OF GOD IS ETERNAL LIFE THROUGH JESUS CHRIST OUR LORD.

KJV

APPENDIX – Verse 13

Reference Scriptures for Verse 13

[R-1] Gal 3:16
Col 1:27
[R-2] 2 Pet 1:4
[R-3] Jn 14:6

Gal 3:16

¹⁶N<small>OW TO</small> A<small>BRAHAM AND HIS SEED WERE THE PROMISES MADE.</small> H<small>E SAITH NOT,</small> A<small>ND TO SEEDS, AS OF MANY; BUT AS OF ONE,</small> A<small>ND TO THY SEED, WHICH IS</small> C<small>HRIST.</small>

KJV

Col 1:27

²⁷T<small>O WHOM</small> G<small>OD WOULD MAKE KNOWN WHAT IS THE RICHES OF THE GLORY OF THIS MYSTERY AMONG THE</small> G<small>ENTILES; WHICH IS</small> C<small>HRIST IN YOU, THE HOPE OF GLORY:</small>

KJV

2 Pet 1:4

⁴W<small>HEREBY ARE GIVEN UNTO US EXCEEDING GREAT AND PRECIOUS PROMISES: THAT BY THESE YE MIGHT BE PARTAKERS OF THE DIVINE NATURE, HAVING ESCAPED THE CORRUPTION THAT IS IN THE WORLD THROUGH LUST.</small>

KJV

Jn 14:6

⁶Jesus saith unto him, I am the way, the truth, and the life: no man cometh unto the Father, but by me.

KJV

APPENDIX – Verse 14

Reference Scriptures for Verse 14

[R-1] 2 Pet 1:4
[R-2] Jn 9:31
[R-2] Lk 22:42

2 Pet 1:4

⁴WHEREBY ARE GIVEN UNTO US EXCEEDING GREAT AND PRECIOUS PROMISES: THAT BY THESE YE MIGHT BE PARTAKERS OF THE DIVINE NATURE, HAVING ESCAPED THE CORRUPTION THAT IS IN THE WORLD THROUGH LUST.

KJV

Jn 9:31

³¹NOW WE KNOW THAT GOD HEARETH NOT SINNERS: BUT IF ANY MAN BE A WORSHIPPER OF GOD, AND DOETH HIS WILL, HIM HE HEARETH.

KJV

Lk 22:42

⁴²SAYING, FATHER, IF THOU BE WILLING, REMOVE THIS CUP FROM ME: NEVERTHELESS NOT MY WILL, BUT THINE, BE DONE.

KJV

APPENDIX – Verse 15

No References or Footnotes

APPENDIX – Verse 16a

Reference Scriptures for Verse 16a

[R-1] Lk 12:48
[R-2] Jn 20:23
[R-3] Jn 10:10

Lk 12:48

⁴⁸BUT HE THAT KNEW NOT, AND DID COMMIT THINGS WORTHY OF STRIPES, SHALL BE BEATEN WITH FEW STRIPES. FOR UNTO WHOMSOEVER MUCH IS GIVEN, OF HIM SHALL BE MUCH REQUIRED: AND TO WHOM MEN HAVE COMMITTED MUCH, OF HIM THEY WILL ASK THE MORE.

KJV

Jn 20:23

²³WHOSE SOEVER SINS YE REMIT, THEY ARE REMITTED UNTO THEM; AND WHOSE SOEVER SINS YE RETAIN, THEY ARE RETAINED.

KJV

Jn 10:10

¹⁰THE THIEF COMETH NOT, BUT FOR TO STEAL, AND TO KILL, AND TO DESTROY: I AM COME THAT THEY MIGHT HAVE LIFE, AND THAT THEY MIGHT HAVE IT MORE ABUNDANTLY.

KJV

APPENDIX – Verse 16b

Reference Scriptures for Verse 16b

[R-1] Matt 12:50
[R-2] Jn 20:23
[R-3] Heb 6:4-6

Matt 12:50

⁵⁰FOR WHOSOEVER SHALL DO THE WILL OF MY FATHER WHICH IS IN HEAVEN, THE SAME IS MY BROTHER, AND SISTER, AND MOTHER.

KJV

Jn 20:23

²³WHOSE SOEVER SINS YE REMIT, THEY ARE REMITTED UNTO THEM; AND WHOSE SOEVER SINS YE RETAIN, THEY ARE RETAINED.

KJV

Heb 6:4-6

⁴FOR IT IS IMPOSSIBLE FOR THOSE WHO WERE ONCE ENLIGHTENED, AND HAVE TASTED OF THE HEAVENLY GIFT, AND WERE MADE PARTAKERS OF THE HOLY GHOST,

⁵AND HAVE TASTED THE GOOD WORD OF GOD, AND THE POWERS OF THE WORLD TO COME,

⁶IF THEY SHALL FALL AWAY, TO RENEW THEM AGAIN UNTO REPENTANCE; SEEING THEY

Appendix – Verse 16b

CRUCIFY TO THEMSELVES THE SON OF GOD AFRESH, AND PUT HIM TO AN OPEN SHAME.
KJV

APPENDIX – Verse 17

Reference Scriptures for Verse 17

[R-1] Lk 5:24
[R-2] Rom 6:23
[R-1] Jn 20:23

Lk 5:24

²⁴BUT THAT YE MAY KNOW THAT *THE SON OF MAN HATH POWER UPON EARTH TO FORGIVE SINS*, (HE SAID UNTO THE SICK OF THE PALSY,) I SAY UNTO THEE, ARISE, AND TAKE UP THY COUCH, AND GO INTO THINE HOUSE.

KJV

Rom 6:23

²³FOR THE WAGES OF SIN IS DEATH; BUT THE GIFT OF GOD IS ETERNAL LIFE THROUGH JESUS CHRIST OUR LORD.

KJV

Jn 20:23

²³WHOSE SOEVER SINS YE REMIT, THEY ARE REMITTED UNTO THEM; AND WHOSE SOEVER SINS YE RETAIN, THEY ARE RETAINED.

KJV

APPENDIX - Verse 18

Reference Scriptures for Verse 18

[R-1] Heb 5:5
[R-1] Heb 11:7
[R] Rev 18:9

Heb 5:5

⁵So also Christ glorified not himself to be made an high priest; but he that said unto him, Thou art my Son, to day have I begotten thee.

KJV

Heb 11:7

⁷By faith Noah, being warned of God of things not seen as yet, moved with fear, prepared an ark to the saving of his house; by the which he condemned the world, and became heir of the righteousness which is by faith.

KJV

Rev 18:9

⁹And the kings of the earth, who have committed fornication and lived deliciously with her, shall bewail her, and lament for her, when they shall see the smoke of her burning,

KJV

APPENDIX – Verse 19

Reference Scriptures for Verse 19

[R-1] Matt 12:43
[R-2] Rev 18:9
[R-3] Jn 14:6, Rev 3:14
[R-4] Col 1:8
[R-5] 1 Tim 6:15

Matt 12:43

⁴³WHEN THE UNCLEAN SPIRIT IS GONE OUT OF A MAN, HE WALKETH THROUGH DRY PLACES, SEEKING REST, AND FINDETH NONE.

KJV

Rev 18:9

⁹AND THE KINGS OF THE EARTH, WHO HAVE COMMITTED FORNICATION AND LIVED DELICIOUSLY WITH HER, SHALL BEWAIL HER, AND LAMENT FOR HER, WHEN THEY SHALL SEE THE SMOKE OF HER BURNING,

KJV

Jn 14:6

⁶JESUS SAITH UNTO HIM, I AM THE WAY, THE TRUTH, AND THE LIFE: NO MAN COMETH UNTO THE FATHER, BUT BY ME.

KJV

Rev 3:14

¹⁴AND UNTO THE ANGEL OF THE CHURCH OF THE LAODICEANS WRITE; THESE THINGS SAITH THE AMEN, THE FAITHFUL AND TRUE WITNESS, THE BEGINNING OF THE CREATION OF GOD;

KJV

Col 1:8

⁸WHO ALSO DECLARED UNTO US YOUR LOVE IN THE SPIRIT.

KJV

1 Tim 6:15

¹⁵WHICH IN HIS TIMES HE SHALL SHEW, WHO IS THE BLESSED AND ONLY POTENTATE, THE KING OF KINGS, AND LORD OF LORDS.

KJV

APPENDIX - Verse 20

Reference Scriptures for Verse 20

[R-1] Jn 8:32
[R-2] Lk 17:21
[R-3] 1 Tim 6:15

Jn 8:32

³²AND YE SHALL KNOW THE TRUTH, AND THE TRUTH SHALL MAKE YOU FREE.

KJV

Lk 17:21

²¹NEITHER SHALL THEY SAY, LO HERE! OR, LO THERE! FOR, BEHOLD, THE KINGDOM OF GOD IS WITHIN YOU.

KJV

1 Tim 6:15

¹⁵WHICH IN HIS TIMES HE SHALL SHEW, WHO IS THE BLESSED AND ONLY POTENTATE, THE KING OF KINGS, AND LORD OF LORDS;

KJV

APPENDIX - Verse 21

Reference Scriptures for Verse 21

[R] Ex 14:7

Ex 14:7

⁷AND HE TOOK SIX HUNDRED CHOSEN CHARIOTS, AND ALL THE CHARIOTS OF EGYPT, AND CAPTAINS OVER EVERY ONE OF THEM.

KJV

TABLE OF REFERENCES

Table of References

1

1 Chron 3:16-17 54
1 Cor 10:4................................. 65
1 Cor 15:3-4 .... 32, 73
1 Cor 15:4............................ 13, 23
1 Cor 15:45.......................... 13, 23
1 Cor 15:47............................... 33
1 Ki 8:25 .... 59, 60
1 Thess 2:1 17
1 Thess 2:11 76
1 Tim 2:5 .... 16, 71
1 Tim 6:15 .... 20, 37, 89, 90

2

2 Chron 36:8-9 54
2 Pet 1:4...................... 18, 79, 81

A

Acts 17:28 .... 16, 63

C

Col 1:27 .... 17, 18, 78, 79
Col 1:8 .... 20, 89
Col 2:10 .... 13, 17, 23, 31, 75

D

Dan 2:45.................................. 64
Dan 7:13............................. 35, 67
Dan 7:14.................................. 67
Dan 7:9........................ 16, 37, 63

E

Ex 14:7 .... 20, 91
Ex 20:1-17 .... 14, 42
Ex 3:2 38
Ex 33:22 64

Ex 7:14-18.......................... 17, 74
Ez 1:2 54

G

Gal 3:16 15, 16, 18, 48, 71, 73, 79
Gal 4:6 .... 16, 70
Gen 1:27................................... 27
Gen 2:21-22............................. 29
Gen 2:22................................... 25
Gen 28:10-14............................ 72
Gen 3:2-6................................. 25
Gen 3:4-5.................................. 27
Gen 3:6-7.................................. 27
Gen 4:1..................................... 28
Gen 49:10................................. 58

H

Heb 11:7 .... 19, 87
Heb 12:2 .... 14, 46
Heb 2:16 52
Heb 4:14 .... 16, 62
Heb 5:5 .... 19, 87
Heb 6:4-6........................... 19, 84

I

Isa 1:18 37

J

Jas 1:21................................... 71
Jer 22:24................................. 54
Jer 22:28-30............................ 54
Jer 22:29-30............................ 55
Jer 22:30........................... 53, 55
Jn 1:17 .... 15, 48
Jn 10:10 .... 18, 83
Jn 10:28 .... 17, 78
Jn 14:6 .... 18, 20, 80, 88

Jn 17:3 .... 17, 77
Jn 20:23 .... 18, 19, 83, 84, 86
Jn 6:54 .... 17, 77
Jn 8:32 .... 20, 90
Jn 9:31 .... 18, 81

L

Lk 1:26-33 68
Lk 12:48 .... 18, 83
Lk 13:32 31
Lk 17:21 .... 20, 90
Lk 22:42 .... 18, 81
Lk 3:2 48
Lk 3:23 .... 15, 16, 49, 70
Lk 3:31 50
Lk 5:21 36
Lk 5:24 .... 19, 86

M

Mal 1:2-3 .... 14, 42
Matt 1:11-12 54
Matt 1:11-16 52
Matt 1:18 51
Matt 1:19 52
Matt 12:43 .... 20, 88
Matt 12:50 .... 19, 84
Matt 19:28 .... 13, 24

Matt 2:2 50
Mk 2:7 36
Mk 5.32-34 34

P

Pet 1:4 18
Pro 24:3 16
Pro 9:1 .... 16, 66
Prov 24:3 63
Prov 9:1 .... 62, 64

R

Rev 12:5 .... 14, 38, 45, 55
Rev 12:9 28
Rev 18:9 .... 19, 20, 87, 88
Rev 19:13 .... 16, 62
Rev 2:8 30
Rev 20:2 28
Rev 22:13 35
Rev 3:14 .... 20, 89
Rom 11:20 .... 14, 47
Rom 6:23 .... 17, 19, 78, 86
Rom 8:15 .... 16, 70

S

Song 2:9 66

About The Author

Sheila R. Vitale is the Spiritual Leader, Founding Teacher, and Pastor of Living Epistles Ministries (*LEM*) and Christ-Centered Kabbalah (*CCK*). A brief history of Pastor Vitale and the unique two-pronged ministry that the Lord Jesus Christ gave her charge over (*LEM/CCK*) is encapsulated below

She moves in the offices of Teacher of Apostolic Doctrine, Prophet, Evangelist and Pastor, has an international following, and has been expounding on the Scripture through a unique spiritual lens for nearly three decades. She has written more than 50 books based on the Old and New Testaments including *The Kabbalah of The 1st Epistle of John* and *the Crime of the Calf* (OT) and *The Three Israels* and *Jesus and The Learned Jew* (NT*)*. She has also rendered original spiritual interpretations of Biblical texts such as *The Prophesies of Daniel According to Kabbalah, Chapter 11,* and *The Noah Chronicles*. Her unique, Multi-Part Message style is seen in *CCK* Serial Messages such as Reincarnation vs Transmigration (22 Parts) and Exodus, Chapter 32 (26 Parts). Each Part of a Multi-Part Message Series can also be enjoyed as a complete and independent study. In addition, she has defined, explained, illustrated and demonstrated hundreds of spiritual principles throughout more than 1,000 CCK lectures.

Her signature work, however, is the three volumes of *The Alternate Translation Bible (ATB)*: *The Alternate Translation Of The Old Testament*, *The Alternate Translation of the New Testament* and *The Alternate Translation of The Book of Revelation*. *The Alternate Translation Bible* is a work in progress (*The ATB Project*). Accordingly, additional spiritual interpretations of both whole and partial Chapters are added from time to time, as they are rendered. The most up-to-date versions of *The ATB Project* may be found online at the *LEM and CCK* websites: *LivingEpistles.org and Christ-CenteredKabbalah.org*, respectively. *The ATB* is a *spiritual interpretation* of the Scripture and is not intended to replace traditional translations.

She also analyzed the Greek text of *The Book of Revelation* and preached extensively on it in the early years of *The ATB Project*. During that time she produced 197 distinct *Message Parts*, under 29 specific *Message Titles*, all of which deal with *The Book of Revelation*.

Pastor Vitale is an illustrator of spiritual principles, a researcher, a translator and a reviewer of the Modern Social Trends of Family and Culture, as they are revealed through TV programs (*The Sopranos), *movies (*The Matrix* and *The Edge of Tomorrow)*, and plays (*Wicked)*. She also writes for the CCK *Blog*.

She travels domestically, as well as internationally, preaching and teaching Judeo-Christian Spiritual Philosophy, and has donated Audio Message Libraries of her Lectures to ministries in Asia, Africa, Europe and North America.

Pastor Vitale serves *CCK* in a range of spiritual, educational, and administrative functions from *The Selden Centre*, *LEM/CCK* headquarters in Selden, New York. She is also a philanthropic individual who supports the *Lighthouse Mission (Patchogue, NY) and HGM – Mission of Hope – Haiti, and other* charitable organizations. She also supports community services such as the *Terryville Fire Department*.

In her spare time, Pastor Vitale enjoys watching movies, attending plays and partaking of cuisines from different cultures. An avid traveler, she has visited several countries in Europe and Africa as well as many cities in the United States.

BEGINNINGS, INSPIRATION AND CALLING

Pastor Vitale began her spiritual journey as a child when her Jewish mother enrolled her in the Hebrew school of an Orthodox synagogue. She experienced the Spirit of God for the first time there in such a profound way that she wept. But after that, when she was only eleven years old, she became very ill and was taken to Mount Sinai Hospital in New York City. She almost died there and has battled with life-threatening health issues ever since. Nevertheless, a deep longing for God continued to pursue her until several years later when she desperately wanted to attend Yeshiva (Jewish high school), but could not. Her secular parents approved of her choice but were not able to afford the tuition.

Much later, after years of searching, she once again experienced the Spirit that had brought her to tears in the synagogue of her youth, but this time it was at *Gospel Revivals Ministries*, a Pentecostal church where Deliverance Ministry was emphasized. She desired to understand the Bible since she was a child, but Scripture was difficult for her and she struggled with the text. Nevertheless, she read one Chapter of the Bible every day until, one day, *her spiritual eyes opened* and she saw an angel holding a little book.

After that, she attended as many as five teaching services each week for about seven years, the latter part of which she edited *Pastor Holzhauser's* books. But several more years had to pass before *the eyes of her understanding opened even further* and she began to receive *Revelation Knowledge of the Scripture*. She understood at that time that the angel she had seen was the angel of Revelation 10:8.

After about seven years of learning *Deliverance Ministry* and *The Doctrine of Sonship* (*Bill Britton*) from *Pastor Holzhauser,* she studied the Bible independently under the influence and direction of the Holy Spirit.

In **1988** she began teaching Apostolic Doctrine.

In **1990** she spent three months in Stony Brook Hospital where she recovered from an incurable disease, defeating premature death, once again, and went on to resume teaching and managing *LEM*.

In **1992** she journeyed to Africa for the first time where she was called to the office of Evangelist.

In the **mid-1990s,** she began to Pastor in addition to being a Teacher of Apostolic Doctrine, a Prophet and an Evangelist, thus, satisfying all five offices of *The Ministry of the Lord Jesus Christ to His Church*.

LIVING EPISTLES MINISTRIES

Pastor Vitale was happy fellowshipping at *Gospel Revivals Ministries* but, eventually, she desired a deeper and more spiritual understanding of the Word of God. One day, after crying out to Jesus about her need, she was amazed to hear Him ask her if she would teach. Her initial response was that she did not see how it would be possible since she was already working a full-time job, despite her poor health. But after the Lord asked her for a second and then a third time, she reluctantly agreed, believing that He would empower her to do the job. Shortly thereafter, in the latter part of 1987, she began to teach her own brand of Judeo-Christian Spiritual Philosophy.

The Lord Jesus Christ named the work *Living Epistles Ministries* in 1988.

The first *LEM* meetings were casual and spontaneous gatherings of friends and fellow deliverance workers in Pastor Vitale's home. After that, they were held in the business office of one of the brethren. Pastor Vitale delivered her first formal message entitled *The Truth About Witchcraft in January of 1988*, followed by *The Seduction of Eve* in April of the same year. After that, she prepared and taught weekly messages including *Signs of Apostleship* and *Lazarus & The Rich Man*. The meetings eventually increased to two and then three each week.

Sometime after that, she learned that the Lord Jesus Christ was revealing spiritual principles from the Hebrew text of the Old Testament through her teachings, and those spiritual principles helped her to begin to unlock the mysteries of the New Testament, as well. Today she understands that the Scripture is a spiritual document that must be spiritually discerned if it is to be understood correctly, and calls that spiritual understanding **The Doctrine of Christ**.

CHRIST-CENTERED KABBALAH

Another Beginning

After about ten years of teaching *the Doctrine of Christ*, in or about the year 2000, while she was evangelizing in Greenville, South Carolina, the Lord Jesus Christ introduced Pastor Vitale to *Lurian Kabbalah*. At that time, the Spirit of God directed her to read and study the teachings of *Rabbi Luria*, as written by his student, *Chayyim Vital,* in *The Tree of Life: The Palace of Adam Kadmon*. She did not understand the text at first, but continued on, nevertheless, until *the eyes of her understanding opened*.

Shortly thereafter, she began to teach *Lurian Kabbalah* and eventually applied the spiritual principles of that system to her studies in the Old Testament under the *Living Epistles*

Ministries brand. Sometime in or about the year 2001, however, the Lord Jesus Christ named her, then current teachings, Christ-centered Kabbalah *(CCK)*, thereby dividing *Living Epistles Ministries* into two branches, each with its own website and digital representations. Each ministry has its own label, but both also share the *LEM/CCK* moniker.

About CCK

Christ-Centered Kabbalah is a new, vigorous approach to spiritual maturity, ascension and rectification (justification) based on Pastor Vitale's original research in *the Hebrew text of the Torah, the Greek text of the New Testament* and *the Zohar,* one of the foundational books of *Philosophical Kabbalah.*

CCK, an integration of the *Doctrine of Christ* and *Lurian Kabbalah,* two Bible-based philosophical systems, offers a fresh perspective concerning Israel's resurrection and Adam's restoration to a higher estate than the one he fell from.

She has studied the authentic Jewish Kabbalah of several Rabbinic scholars, including *Moses Nachmanides (Ramban), Moses Cordovero (Ramak)* and *Isaac Luria (The Ari) and* has read many of the English translations of their writings, including *Ramban's The Gate of Reward, Ramak's Pardes Rimonim (Orchard of Pomegranates),* and *the* teachings *of the Ari,* as written by his student, *Chayyim Vital*: *The Gate of Reincarnations* and *The Tree of Life: The Palace of Adam Kadmon.* Pastor Vitale attributes her ability to understand and teach authentic *Jewish Kabbalah* and *Christ-Centered Kabbalah,* which she believes is beyond the grasp of the human mind, to *The Lord Jesus Christ.*

Pastor Vitale cautions her students about the dangers of *Occult Qabalah* and warns everyone with ears to hear that all Kabbalah is not kosher (authentic). Pastor Vitale teaches *authentic Jewish Kabbalah, which glorifies God* and shuns the *occult Qabalah of personal power,* which, all too frequently, is used to control unsuspecting persons, acquire wealth by spiritual power, or punish one's enemies.

Media

CCK publishes a wide range of material, including books, e-books, spiritual interpretations of the Scripture and transcripts of Pastor Vitale's *Christ-Centered Kaballah* Lectures. Many of her transcripts and the entire *Alternate Translation Bible* may be viewed without charge on the *CCK Website* (*Christ-CenteredKaballah.org*).

She also has an *Author's Website* where all of her books, as well as several photographs of herself and a short biography are displayed (Amazon.com/author/SheilaVitale). Paperback and digital versions of *CCK* books may be purchased through *Amazon, Google Books* and *Barnes & Noble. CCK* also provides free videos of her live streams through YouTube: *@Christ-CenteredKabbalah),* and other Internet Plat-forms.

PASTOR VITALE TODAY

Today Pastor Vitale continues to dedicate her life to teaching the spiritual principles of the Bible and focuses daily on studying, writing and preaching powerful messages from *The Selden Centre,* LEM/CCK's headquarters at Selden, New York.

THE COMMON SALVATION

The Book of Jude Unlocked Through Kabbalah

Sheila R. Vitale
Christ-Centered Kabbalah

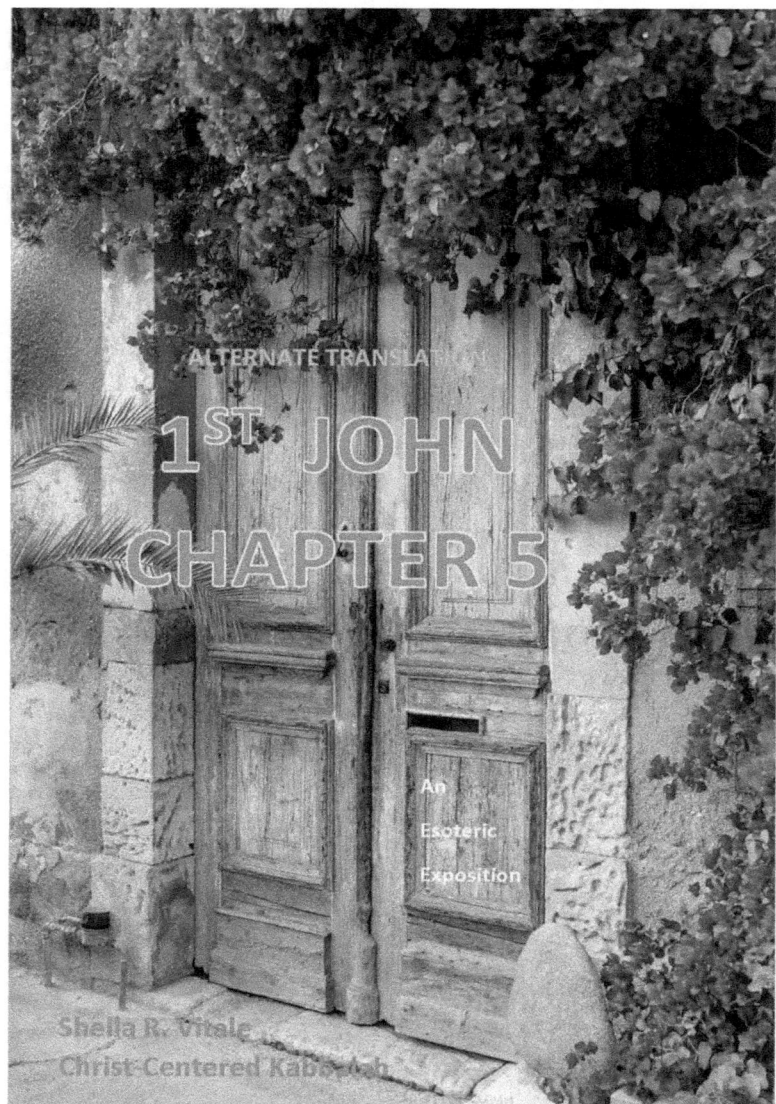

SOPHIA
EXPERIENCING 2ND THESSALONIANS, CHAPTER 2

SHEILA R. VITALE

LIVING EPISTLES MINISTRIES

THE CRIME OF THE CALF

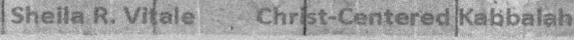

Sheila R. Vitale   Christ-Centered Kabbalah

The Noah Chronicles

An Esoteric Exposition of Noah's Seduction

Including the Alternate Translation of

Genesis 9:18-27

Sheila R. Vitale

Christ-Centered Kabbalah

Christ-Centered Kabbalah
Sheila R Vitale,
Pastor, Teacher & Founder
~ The Compleat Kabbalah ~
PO Box 562, Port Jefferson Station, New York 11776, USA
Christ-CenteredKabbalah.org *or* Books@Christ-CenteredKabbalah.org

www.ingramcontent.com/pod-product-compliance
Lightning Source LLC
Chambersburg PA
CBHW050645160426
43194CB00010B/1820